IMAGES
of America
TUGBOATS ON
PUGET SOUND

Legendary Tugboat. The 128-foot-long steam tugboat *Wanderer*, shown here in the early 1900s towing a square-rigger through Puget Sound, is one of the region's most historically significant workboats. Built in 1890 at the Hall Brothers Shipyard in Port Blakely located across the Sound from Seattle, her size, sweeping design, massive hull, and impressive superstructure typified the powerful tugboats of her era. Because of her heavy wood construction by skilled shipwrights, the *Wanderer's* working life lasted more than a half century before old age coupled with unpredictable weather and sea conditions took their inevitable maritime toll. (Courtesy Puget Sound Maritime Historical Society, No. 2800-57.)

On the Cover: Several vintage tugboats—including, from right to left, *Standfast* (1943), *Palomar* (1912), *Sand Man* (1909), and, on the back, *Bee* (1903)—jockey for position during the 1980 Olympia Harbor Days tugboat races on Budd Inlet. A more-than-three-decade-old maritime heritage-focused festival held on Labor Day weekend, Harbor Days is a tribute to the tugboats of Puget Sound and British Columbia, which were a vital part of the region's colorful maritime history. (Courtesy Scott Schoch.)

TUGBOATS ON PUGET SOUND

To Tom Crowley

Chuck Fowler and Capt. Mark Freeman

Chuck Fowler

Mark Freeman

ISBN 978-0-7385-5972-5

Published by Arcadia Publishing
Charleston SC, Chicago IL, Portsmouth NH, San Francisco CA

Printed in the United States of America

Library of Congress Catalog Card Number: 2008930909

For all general information contact Arcadia Publishing at:
Telephone 843-853-2070
Fax 843-853-0044
E-mail sales@arcadiapublishing.com
For customer service and orders:
Toll-Free 1-888-313-2665

Visit us on the Internet at www.arcadiapublishing.com

To the late Franz Schlottmann, longtime owner, skipper, and steward of the historic Puget Sound tugboat Sand Man *and to Robin and Kae Paterson, tireless ambassadors for tugs, old and new.*

CONTENTS

ACKNOWLEDGMENTS

Although some coauthors who write and edit a book may find it a difficult and contentious process, creating Images of America: *Tugboats on Puget Sound* has been a labor of workboat love. Building on an almost 30-year friendship, the development of this particular book has been one of mutual respect and complementary collaboration. Mark is the real tugboat company owner, tug captain and master, hands-on historian, and conscientious collector of tugboat photographs, information, and artifacts. I am the tugboat enthusiast, wannabe captain who is a hands-on maritime historian, researcher, journalist, and teller of tugboat tales.

Creating a book about tugboats is not a singular task. Mark and I could not have produced this book without the dedicated help of many others. Among these people are my colleagues in the Puget Sound Maritime Historical Society, Jack Carver, Nat Howe, Karl House, Ron Chaput, and Ron Burke. The society is the maritime affiliate of the Seattle's Museum of History and Industry (MOHAI) whose librarian, Carolyn Marr, and photograph technician, Kathleen Knies, provided excellent assistance. Other professionals who helped find and reproduce often illusive images were Nicolette Bromberg, University of Washington Libraries Special Collections; Christina Burtner, University of Washington (UW) Classroom Support Services Photography; Elaine Miller, Washington State Historical Society; Lorraine Scott, Bainbridge Island Historical Society and Museum; Marsha Moratti, Jefferson County Historical Society Research Center; Robert Schuler, Tacoma Public Library; and Bill Kooiman, J. Porter Shaw Library, San Francisco Maritime National Historical Park. Three tugboat and maritime industry representatives in Seattle provided valued access to their company photograph archives: Mike Skalley, Foss Maritime Company; Jim Van der Veen, Crowley, Maritime Corporation; and Lisa Haug, Manson Construction Company. Also the late Drew and Henryetta "Tooty" Foss Hager, my valued friends during the past decade, helped preserve the colorful tugboat history chronicled in these pages.

Several of our tugboat owner and industry friends deserve Mark's and my deepest appreciation—first among them are Robin Paterson and his wife and tug mate, Kae. We also want to thank our wives, Karla Fowler and Margie Freeman, for without their encouragement and support this book would not have been possible.

Mark especially values the late Joe Williamson, who helped him start his maritime photograph collection at an early age, as well as Jim Cary, Pat and Merry Stoppleman, Mark Gilkey, Jack Wyatt, Jay Peterson, Thom Davies, Bob Shrewsbury Sr., Bob and Ric Shrewsbury, and John Benthien for their photographs, information, and continuing support. Because of limited space, Mark can only offer his sincere thank you to all who have shared their photographs and stories through the decades.

Finally, we appreciate the following professionals at Arcadia Publishing for their cooperation and understanding: Sarah Higginbotham, Julie Albright, Devon Weston, Christine Talbot, Julie Rivers, Lynn Ruggieri, and other staff members.

INTRODUCTION

In the United States, the history of magnificent ocean-going, square-rigged ships and grand passenger steamers is well known. However, the story of tugboats, the tough, powerful workboats that assisted these vessels in and out of harbors and performed many other marine support duties, has received comparatively little attention. These workhorses of the maritime industry have labored long in the shadows of their larger, more impressive nautical neighbors—from the square-riggers, steam ships, and mighty battleships of the past to the cavernous aircraft carriers, cruise liners, and container ships of today. Because of its traditional "can do" maritime business context, distinctly designed workboats, colorful captains, and intrepid crews, tugboat history deserves greater recognition. And in the Pacific Northwest and Washington state's Puget Sound, this proud heritage is a significant, honored part of the region's robust history.

As Steven Lange and Peter Spectre wrote in their authoritative book, *On the Hawser: A Tugboat Album*, "The tugboat is an indispensable part of our maritime transportation system. Without it, shipping at today's scale and intensity would be impossible. Tugboats allow large ships to be maneuvered in close quarters, barges to be towed . . . and workaday tasks to be performed without delay and with a minimum of inconvenience." The authors conclude by noting, "Yet they are a fairly recent phenomenon in maritime history, having been introduced in the early years of the 19th century."

According to Lange and Spectre, the first practical steamboat, designed to tow barges in Scotland, was built in the early 1800s and followed in 1821 by the steam-paddle tug *Monkey* for the British Navy. Tugboat history in the United States began 18 years after the advent of Robert Fulton's first steamboat, the passenger-carrying *Claremont,* in 1807 when the paddle-wheel tug *Rufus King* was constructed in 1825 for harbor operations in New York City.

When tugboats became numerous on the Atlantic Coast during the following decades, older towboats began making their way to the Pacific Coast after gold was discovered in northern California in 1849 and major westward expansion began. Eventually many of the early tugboats working on San Francisco Bay migrated to Puget Sound as the region's lumber and other natural resource–based businesses developed. This Atlantic to Pacific Coast maritime migration pattern followed that of the early tall sailing ships as the overall development of the West continued.

As noted in Chapter One, "The Beginnings: Tugboats on the Sound," it is widely known that the first steamboat to operate in the Pacific Northwest and Puget Sound was the British Hudson's Bay Company (HBC) paddle wheel–equipped *Beaver* in 1836. And while the venerable steamer was converted in 1874 to a tugboat in British Columbia waters, there are only passing references by historians to her possible occasional use earlier as a towboat during her HBC operations in Puget Sound.

As chronicled in Chapter Two, "Boom, Bust, and Rebound: 1891–1940," the towboat business in Puget Sound, commonly referred to as "the Sound," went through decades of economic growth, depression, and reinvention of the industry from 1891 to 1940. Companies were formed and competed ferociously, and some succeeded while others failed. Smart, crafty tug operators survived and grew, and some smaller businesses were purchased and merged into larger enterprises.

The Fremont Boat Market, and later Fremont Boat Company, as well as Fremont Towboat Company were established during this mercurial economic period. This very personal story is told in Chapter Three, "A Tugboat Family's Story: 1915–2008." Within the broad sweep of Puget Sound tugboat history, it provides a more focused look at a smaller Seattle-based workboat company and the family that built it over a period of more than 90 years.

From the beginning of World War II in 1941 until the late 1970s, Puget Sound tugboat companies large and small found new opportunities. Wartime production included building powerful, specialized tugboats for military use, and after the war these vessels helped modernize the fleets of the regional tug companies. Maritime and other businesses in the Pacific Northwest continued their growth, and, at the end of this period, another new western Gold Rush developed; this time it was black gold (petroleum) with the discovery of major new oil fields in Alaska. The oil discoveries in Alaska required a massive new infrastructure to explore and drill for the new petroleum and transportation systems to and from the Sound. Tugboats, barges, and specialized new equipment were essential parts of this new economic opportunity. This evolving, changing saga is told in Chapter Four, "War, Renewal, and New Business: 1941–1979."

The final Chapter, "The Modern Tugboat Era: 1980–2008," tells the story of how these economic, ownership, and technological developments continued and brought significant change to the tugboat business in Puget Sound. Continually evolving marine transportation needs also brought major tug design, propulsion, and other innovations.

While this book can only provide an overview and brief glimpse into Puget Sound tugboat history, there is another more personal, hands-on way to learn about and experience this fascinating heritage. Beginning in the late 1940s, Seattle, Olympia, and Tacoma helped renew interest in the region's workboat heritage by staging festivals and seemingly improbable but exciting tug races. These events recall the days more than a century ago when steam tugboats would race to meet square-riggers and other cargo sailing ships entering the Sound, with the first boats on the scene usually getting the work to tow them to their destination ports. Such community celebrations showcase both working commercial tugs as well as carefully restored retired workboats whose owners help preserve the region's tugboat heritage. These family-focused events allow people of all ages to actually see and tour tugs, talk with their captains and crew members, and learn firsthand about tugboat history.

Tugboat heritage has been largely hidden from public view nationwide; however in the Pacific Northwest and Puget Sound, it is both accessible and appreciated. This book seeks to honor and recognize some of the individuals, companies, and tugs, and also port cities that helped make this colorful history.

One

The Beginnings
Tugboats on the Sound

Most maritime historians agree that perhaps the most iconic vessel of early European-American maritime history in the Pacific Northwest is the British Hudson Bay Company's (HBC) steamer *Beaver*. For more than half a century in the 1800s, beginning as a trading outpost supply ship and British national presence and ending its long service wrecked onshore as a still utilitarian tugboat, she plied the waters of what became Washington in the United States as well as British Columbia in Canada.

The small steamer's primary purpose was to carry cargo and passengers to and from the HBC's frontier forts and help expand its profitable fur trading–related businesses. But maritime historian Gordon Newell believed that the *Beaver* also did some supplementary towing during its trips in and out of Puget Sound. If so, then in a limited sense the steamer was also the first tugboat on the United States side of the border.

However, as lumber, grain, fish, coal, and other natural resources replaced fur as the region's most valued commodities, special purpose steam tugboats arrived from California—particularly in San Francisco. For the time, these powerful tugs towed engineless cargo sailing ships from the Pacific Ocean to and from the inland seaports of Puget Sound. The big side-wheel tugboats, *Resolute, Cyrus Walker, Politofsky, Goliah, Favorite,* and others, were the first of many that worked throughout the Sound, making names for themselves and money for their owners. These early tugs initiated the region's fascinating, ever-changing tugboat history.

FORERUNNER TUGBOAT. During its later life in Pacific Northwest waters, the first steamboat in the region, the British Hudson's Bay Company (HBC) small steamboat *Beaver*, became both a supply and tugboat as shown above. Built in England, the side paddle wheel *Beaver* began its career in 1836 on the Columbia River and later in Puget Sound and British Columbia. She carried cargo and passengers to the company's forts and trading posts in the region;. however, historians make only passing reference that the *Beaver* might have been used as an occasional tugboat on the Sound during her more than a half century of service before, as seen below, she was wrecked on a rocky shore in Vancouver, British Columbia, in 1888. (Both courtesy Vancouver Maritime Museum, Leonard McCann.)

TRANSPLANTED TUGBOAT. Among several purpose-built tugboats brought to Puget Sound from San Francisco to support the rapidly developing timber milling industry was the 128-foot-long side-wheeler *Cyrus Walker*. Named for the general manager of the Pope and Talbot mill at Port Gamble, the *Walker* arrived in the Sound in 1871 to tow log rafts and sailing ships from the Pacific Ocean to and from the company's mill. (Courtesy Puget Sound Maritime Historical Society [PSMHS].)

RUSSIAN GUNBOAT TUG. As part of the purchase of Alaska by the United States from Russia, the 125-foot-long gunboat *Politofsky* was converted and became a well-known tugboat on Puget Sound. After her long towing career and dismantling in 1897, her large brass steam whistle was ceremoniously sounded by Pres. William Howard Taft to open Seattle's Alaska-Pacific-Yukon Exposition in 1809. (Courtesy Bainbridge Island Historical Society.)

FAVORITE NAME. The name *Favorite* has been given to several Puget Sound tugboats during the past 150 years, but the most widely known was the first. Built as a 125-foot-long side-wheel passenger and cargo steamer at Utsalady on Camano Island in 1869, she was purchased by the Puget Mill Company in 1876. Converted to a tugboat, she worked for two additional owners, the Port Madison and Port Blakely mills, before being dismantled in 1920. (Courtesy PSMHS, No. 952.)

THE GREAT *GOLIAH*. The second tugboat built in the United States in 1849, the 136-foot-long *Goliah*, left its original New York homeport and sailed to San Francisco as a Gold Rush–era passenger and freight steamer and later tug. Purchased in 1871 by Pope and Talbot, the original *Goliah* was brought to Puget Sound to support the company's mill operation at Port Gamble. After many faithful years of towing, she became obsolete and was sold for scrap in 1899. (Courtesy University of Washington [UW] Libraries, Special Collections, No. UW8369.)

Two

Boom, Bust, and Rebound 1891–1940

A new era of the tugboat business on Puget Sound began in 1891 when the Puget Sound Tugboat Company was formed by an association of the region's lumber mill owners and began operation. Instead of the familiar side-wheel steamers of the early days, several new screw propeller–equipped tugs formed the company's core fleet.

Hundreds of big square-riggers, schooners, and other sailing vessels needed tug assistance to bring them through the Sound and to and from lumber mills and other cargo loading and unloading terminals. Also, huge rafts of logs needed to be towed from the vast forests ringing the Sound to busy mills for processing into lumber for expanding economies.

The region's resource-fueled boom times also turned into bust periods in 1893 and, more than three decades later, in 1929. Tugboat companies were not immune to these downturns; some went out of business and others survived and grew.

As wind-powered sailing vessels gave way to steam-powered ships on the Sound in the early 1900s, tugboats shifted their services with the changing technological and economic times. Another period of change came in the 1920s and 1930s when steam engines in tugs were replaced by more efficient diesel power plants.

Smaller but still very competitive tug companies also developed on the Sound as towing businesses grew along with shipping, cargo warehousing and handling, and other related industries. The almost half-century-long period from the 1890s to the beginning of World War II was one of economic growth, retrenchments, and redevelopment for Puget Sound tugboat operations. But hard-working, sea-savvy companies survived, grew, and powered toward new entrepreneurial horizons.

TUG AND TALL SHIP. The steam tugboat *Richard Holyoke* is shown here in the early 1900s tied to the British four-mast square-rigger *Balmoral* at Port Townsend. One of the original four tug fleet of the first large marine towing enterprise, the Puget Sound Tugboat Company, the *Holyoke* was built in Seabeck on Hood Canal in 1877. She had a long towing career on the Sound under several owners before being dismantled on Lake Union in 1935. (Courtesy Jefferson County Historical Society, No. 2.260.)

STEAM AND SAIL. Renowned maritime artist Steve Mayo depicted the powerful-looking *Richard Holyoke*, towing a square-rigger with sails raised, through Pacific Northwest waters. The 115-foot-long tug was one of the first classically designed, screw-propeller tugboats that departed from the less efficient side-and-stern paddle wheel propulsion, and she also survived long enough to be converted from steam to diesel power. (Courtesy Steve Mayo.)

***TYEE* FAST TRANSIT.** In this classic photograph taken in the late 1890s, the 141-foot-long steam tug *Tyee* is shown powering through choppy seas on Puget Sound with spray flying to the sides of her squared-off stem. She was built in 1884 in Port Ludlow for Pope and Talbot's Puget Mill Company by Hiram Doncaster and William McCurdy. The *Tyee* had a 1,000-horsepower steam engine and was claimed to be the most powerful tug in the United States when launched. (Courtesy PSMHS, No. 2575-1.)

Hauled: High and Dry. Large vessels including tugboats require continuing maintenance. In these two photographs taken in the early 1900s, the wooden-hulled *Tyee* has been hauled out at the Hall Brothers Marine Railway and Shipyard in Eagle Harbor on Bainbridge Island. According to the Pope and Talbot company history "Time, Tide, and Timber," when a ship surveyor examined the tug in 1916 after 34 years of hard towing service, he reported that the tug was "staunch, strong, and well-built in every particular." The official survey report stated the *Tyee* still had an exceptionally fine frame and ceiling knees and decks that showed no signs of having strained or worked during her long years of hard service. (Both courtesy UW Libraries, Special Collections; above No. 278692, below No. 278702.)

TYEE WITH SAILS. While early tugboats on the Sound towed square-rigger and other sailing vessels, few casual observers realize that some like the *Tyee* also carried their own sails—steadying sails. As seen in this photograph, two rolled-up sails are apparent: a jib on the bow hanging from the forestay and another behind the stack attached to the aft mast. These steadying sails could reduce a tugboat's roll by up to half in high winds and heavy seas. (Courtesy PSMHS, No. 2575-15.)

TUGBOAT WELCOME. Loaded with well-wishers and decorated or dressed with signal flags, the *Tyee* helps welcome the steamship *Queen* into Seattle's Elliott Bay in 1899. The steamer had just returned from the Philippine Islands with soldiers from the First Washington Volunteer Infantry Regiment, which had helped quell an insurrection. (Courtesy UW Libraries, Special Collections, Wilse No. 66.5.)

BUILDING *WANDERER*. Another of the founding fleet of the Puget Sound Tugboat Company was the legendary *Wanderer*. The famous tug is shown under construction (above) next to a schooner at the Hall Brothers shipyard in Port Blakely prior to being launched (below) in the spring of 1890. Gary White in his book, *Hall Brothers Shipbuilders*, called the *Wanderer* "an unusually graceful but very powerful tug." The *Wanderer* was built for the Port Blakely Mill Company specifically for towing log rafts to the mill as well as sailing vessels to and from the mill. (Both courtesy Brainbridge Island Historical Society; above No. 2147, below No. 2138.)

Festive Tug. Dressed with signal flags and ready to host onboard guests, the *Wanderer* is shown at Port Townsend in 1903 during the city's Independence Day celebration on the Fourth of July. In addition to their heavy towing schedules, the *Wanderer* and other tugs of the Puget Sound Tugboat Company participated in local events in their homeport and other communities around the Sound. (Courtesy PSMHS, No. 2678-31.)

Gauging History. This brass steam-engine revolution counter gauge from the *Wanderer* was removed in 1947 after the Foss Launch and Tug Company tug ran aground in Puget Sound because of foggy weather and swift currents at Double Bluff on Whidbey Island. The gauge, which totaled engine revolutions until the next required maintenance, and other items were preserved. Eventually the historic artifact will be donated to a museum. (Courtesy Chuck Fowler.)

Tall Ship Tow. Two Pacific Towboat Company steam tugs, the *Harold C.* and the *Yellow Jacket*, are shown on Puget Sound in the 1910s. They are towing the three-mast, Norwegian-owned square-rigger *Ganges* to its seaport destination to load cargo. The 66-foot-long *Yellow Jacket* was launched in 1900, and the 55-foot-long *Harold C.* was built in 1903 and later purchased by Foss, converted to diesel power, and renamed the *Foss No. 17.* (Courtesy Museum of History and Industry, No. 83.10.PA7.26.)

GOLIAH TOO. The second tugboat named *Goliah,* shown here towing a square-rigger, was a massive 151-foot-long screw propeller steamer built in Camden, New Jersey, in 1907. She and her sister tug *Hercules* came to San Francisco, and the *Goliah* was purchased by the Puget Sound Tugboat Company in 1909 and brought to the Pacific Northwest. The *Hercules* is now part of the San Francisco Maritime National Historical Park vessel collection at Hyde Street Pier. (Courtesy PSMHS.)

STEAM TUG *TATOOSH.* Launched in 1890 in Seattle at the Moran Shipyard, the steam tug *Tatoosh* was built by the Puget Sound Tugboat Company for the then unheard of cost of $80,000. The 128-foot-long steel-hull tug was heralded as the finest tug on the Pacific Coast at the time of her construction and attained a speed of 14 knots on her sea trial run. (Courtesy PSMHS, No. 3403-8.)

PROUD *PIONEER*. The stout iron-hull tug *Pioneer* was constructed in 1878 in Philadelphia. She was purchased by the Port Discovery Mill in 1887 and by Puget Sound Tugboat Company in 1892. Pope and Talbot bought the tug in 1926 and sold her to Foss in 1949. (Courtesy PSMHS, No. 1935.)

SMOKIN' *SEA LION*. Shown showing off her best to her onboard guests and dressed with signal flags, the 107-foot-long *Sea Lion* steams through Puget Sound in the early 1900s. She was built in Camden, New Jersey, and had been owned and operated briefly in 1909 by the Puget Sound Tugboat Company until she was struck by a sailing schooner and sank in foggy weather. (Courtesy PSMHS, No. 2948-5.)

STERN STYLE. The unmistakable design and style of a classic Puget Sound workboat is apparent in this early 1900s view of the stern of the tug *Alice*. Built as a steam-powered fish cannery tender in 1892 for the Pacific Packing and Navigation Company, she was later sold and operated as a tugboat by two companies before being purchased in 1919 by Foss Launch and Tug Company and renamed *Foss No. 18*. (Courtesy PSMHS, No. 1159-1.)

SAND MAN AND STEAMERS. The tugboat *Sand Man* is shown at left in this 1910 photograph across from passenger steamers at Percival's Dock on the Olympia waterfront. The stern-wheeler *Multnomah* is shown in the foreground with the steamers *S. G. Simpson* and *Greyhound* approaching the dock. Built by Crawford and Reid in Tacoma in 1909, the *Sand Man* has survived for almost 100 years and is an icon of Olympia maritime history. (Courtesy UW Libraries, Special Collections, A. Curtis No. 20621.)

IMPOSING CREW. The crew of the steam tugboat *Favorite* strikes a pose in front of her classically designed wheelhouse in this early 1900s photograph taken on the Seattle waterfront. Tugs of various sizes, power, and capabilities were a familiar part of the growing city's expanding maritime industry as ship assisting and other various towing assignments kept the workboats busy in the late 1800s and early 1900s. (Courtesy UW Libraries, Special Collections, No. 27.871z.)

Twin Tugs. The Blekum Towboat Company's two steam tugs *Mystic* and *Oscar B.* are shown on the Seattle waterfront in 1910. The 50-foot-long *Mystic* was built in Eagle Harbor on Bainbridge Island in 1891, and the 58-foot-long *Oscar B.* was built in 1897 in Tacoma as a passenger steamer and was converted to a tug, which later became the *Rouse* and then *Wallace Foss* when purchased by Foss Launch and Tug Company in 1920. (Courtesy PSMHS, No. 1083-2.)

Waterfront Wharf Scene. Three types of transportation are shown in this photograph of the Seattle waterfront taken about 1917. The classically designed steam tug *Magic* is tied to a float at right, and a steam ship and a Model T Ford are seen at the wharf on the left. The 67-foot-long *Magic* was built at Port Blakely in 1893 and almost reached her half-century anniversary before she was abandoned in 1942. (Courtesy PSMHS, No. 1477-2.)

STEAMER CONVERSION. The passenger steamer *Audrey*, shown above, was one of many boats on Puget Sound that was converted to a tugboat in her later maritime life. After her launch in Tacoma in 1909, she served as a passenger steamer and later as a grocery store boat operating between Tacoma, Anderson Island, and various Key Peninsula stops and later became a shrimp trawler. It was sold to the Delta V. Smyth Tug and Barge Company of Olympia in 1942. The *Audrey* was repowered with a diesel engine and towed in the south Sound until 1960 when Foss Launch and Tug bought the Smyth business. Declared surplus by Foss, she was sold again in 1963 and eventually scrapped in Bellingham. (Both courtesy Robin Paterson.)

TUGBOAT CHANGEOVER. Another south Sound steamer, the 50-foot-long *Mizpah*, is shown above around 1910 when she was carrying passengers, freight, and mail from Olympia to various Carr Inlet communities in the south Sound. She was launched in 1905 and served for 10 years as a passenger steamer before she burned to the waterline in 1915 and was converted to a tugboat, seen below, for the Capital City Tug Company owned by Volney Young. She was repowered with a diesel engine in 1922 and became one of the first such motor tugs on the Sound. The *Mizpah* was purchased in 1947 by O. H. "Doc" Freeman and, among other uses, his teenage son Mark operated her while learning the towing business. (Both courtesy Robin Paterson.)

TALE OF THE *TILLICUM*. The steam tugboat *Tillicum* is shown at left lying or moored at the Stimson Mill dock in Seattle's Ballard neighborhood in 1904. Built in 1901 by Thomas Reed for the company, the tug was used to tow logs to the mill and also ships to be loaded with lumber. She was sold to American Tugboat Company in Everett in 1916, and a diesel engine was installed in 1940. Bob Waterman purchased the *Tillicum* about 1960, and he towed with her for 25 years. The photograph below shows the venerable tug in Olympia during Harbor Days where in 1988 she was named the event's honored "logo" tug. Unfortunately, shortly afterward, the more than 80-year-old tug sank in Tacoma. (At left, courtesy UW Libraries, Special Collections, A. Curtis No. 04259-8; below, Karla Fowler.)

Tug Rescue. The tug *Simpson* stands ready to help rescue passengers who were aboard the Puget Sound Mosquito Fleet steamer *Florence J.* during a launching accident in 1914 at Dockton on Maury Island. Onboard guests, dressed in special occasion clothing, are seen scrambling to safety from the sinking steamer's cabin and onto nearby floats and also the tug. (Courtesy UW Libraries, Special Collections, No. CUR351.)

Tall Ship and Tug Wreck. Tall ships as well as tugs often met their final demise grounded and wrecked near shore. Here the British Columbia tug *Lorne*, built in 1889, and the former sailing ship *America*, which was converted to a coal cargo barge, are seen on the rocks at False Bay, San Juan Island, in 1914. While the ship barge was a total loss, the strongly built *Lorne* was refloated, repaired, and continued towing until scrapped in 1937. (Courtesy PSMHS, No. 2628-2.)

EQUATOR IN ACTION. Once chartered for a South Pacific voyage by famous *Treasure Island* author Robert Louis Stevenson when it was rigged for sail, the *Equator* had a long history. Built in 1888 in Benica, California, as a two-mast, 81-foot-long schooner, the *Equator* was converted to a steam-powered tug as shown in the photograph above and later converted to diesel. Purchased and brought to Puget Sound by the Cary-Davis Tugboat Company, she was part of the Puget Sound Tug and Barge fleet and is shown below towing the schooner barge *Sandy* in the 1920s. The remains of the *Equator*'s hull are on exhibit near Everett's Marina Park. (Both courtesy PSMHS; above No. 903-32, below 903-9.)

MONARCH OF THE SEAS. The *Sea Monarch* was one of several 150-foot-long, 1,000-horsepower steam tugboats built during World War I for military support service by the U.S. Shipping Board. Four of these wooden tugs built in Oakland, California, were uncompleted at the end of the war, and, in 1922, Thomas Crowley bought all four. He fitted out and sent the *Sea Monarch* (above) to Seattle to work for Cary-Davis (below), a tug company in which he had a financial interest. This began Crowley towing operations in Puget Sound and the north Pacific, which has become one of the company's major maritime business markets. (Both courtesy Mark Freeman.)

TUG TRANSFORMATION. Built in 1908 for the Olympic Tug and Barge Company, the steam tugboat *Olympian* towed for more than half a century on the Sound. Along with the *Elf* and *Echo*, the *Olympian* was sold to Foss in 1916. Renamed *Foss No. 16* (above), her deck cabin was cut open to accommodate her conversion from steam to diesel engine power. The company's "breadwinner" tug in the 1920s, after 55 years of constant towing (below) and two diesel engine changes, *Foss No. 16* was laid up permanently in 1963. She was sold to a private owner but sank and was turned over to the Divers Institute of Seattle to be raised and used as a salvage training vessel. (Above, courtesy Foss Maritime; below, Mark Freeman.)

THE REAL "TUGBOAT ANNIE." Although Tugboat Annie was the name of a fictional magazine and later a movie character, there was a real steam tugboat on Puget Sound with a similar name. Built in 1914 by Portland Shipbuilding Company, the *Anne W.*, shown above under full power, had very shallow draft or underwater hull depth and a tunnel propeller for river towing. Following her river service in Oregon, she was used successfully offshore in difficult Alaskan waters, which was very uncommon for a shallow draft riverboat. The *Anne W.* was purchased in 1927 by Pioneer Sand and Gravel to move barges to and from its gravel pit mine in Steilacoom, as shown below, to its operations in Tacoma, Seattle and other terminals in the Sound. (Above, courtesy PSMHS, No. 191-12; below, Tacoma Public Library, Richards No. D45392-37.)

FIRST DIESEL-POWERED TUG. The first full diesel-powered tugboat in the United States was the *Chickamauga*, shown here underway in the 1920s. Named after Lake Chickamauga in Wisconsin, she was launched in 1915 in Seattle and was powered by a 240-horsepower Nelsco diesel, a German-developed engine built under license in the United States. In 1929, she became part of the Puget Sound Tug and Barge towing operation. She was later owned by a Foss company and survives today as a live-aboard in Seattle's Lake Union. (Courtesy PSMHS, No. 499-13.)

OLYMPIA TOWING COMPANY TUGS. Three tugboats of the Olympia Towing Company fleet are shown moored at the company's dock in the 1930s. From left to right are the tugs *Klatawa*, *Leonine*, and the *Nemah*. Established in 1927 by Milton Willie and a partner, the business was run by Willie family members for three generations before its sale to Dunlap Towing of La Conner in 1989. (Courtesy Mark Freeman.)

Tight Tug Tow. The American Tugboat Company's diesel tug *Irene*, at left in the photograph above, is shown alongside the steam tug *Mary D. Hume* as she tows a massive snaking log raft outbound through the narrow, always challenging Deception Pass in north Puget Sound in the late 1940s. The *Hume* was built in late 1881 in Oregon as a steam-powered cannery schooner and a whaler for a short time and finally a tugboat in 1908 when purchased by American Tugboat Company. The *Irene* towed for the Everett-based American until sold and later resold to Crowley in 1973. The tug was sold to private owners for recreational cruising, and she is still operating on the Sound. The *Hume* was donated to a historical society in Oregon to be preserved as a historic tug, but the project failed. (Both courtesy Mark Freeman.)

Foss Tug Lineup, 1931. Established in 1889 in Tacoma by Andrew and Thea Foss, the Foss Launch and Tug Company had the largest tugboat fleet in Puget Sound when this photograph was taken in 1931. Shown above are 12 tugs and a utility boat (far right) lined up in front of the office on Dock Street. From left to right, large to small, are the 97-foot-long *Andrew Foss*, built in 1905; *Foss No. 21*; *Foss No. 18*; *Foss No. 16*; *Peter Foss*; *Justine Foss*; *Foss No. 17*; *Rosedale*,

later renamed *Grace Foss; Henrietta Foss; Rustler; Foss No. 12: Diamond B.*; and the 32-foot-long *Peggy Foss*. The floating Foss office at Dock Street burned four months after this photograph was taken; it was rebuilt at the same site until towed to its current F Street location in 1943. (Courtesy Tacoma Public Library, Boland No. 10435.)

TUGBOATS AND THE *CONSTITUTION*. After a comprehensive restoration, the frigate USS *Constitution* was towed to port communities throughout the United States for public commemorations in 1933. Built in 1787 in Boston and still the oldest-commissioned ship in the U.S. Navy, the historic ship visited Puget Sound and was towed and escorted by Foss tugs during its tour. She is shown above being escorted through the Tacoma Narrows by the *Peter Foss* and towed by *Foss No. 18* hidden on the far side of the ship. Then a teenager, Drew Foss was aboard the *Peter* during this memorable tow to Olympia and back. During its tow along the Seattle waterfront by the converted U.S. Navy minesweeper *Grebe*, off to the right in the photograph below, the famous frigate was escorted by, from left to right, *Harbor Patrol No. 1*, *Foss No. 19*, and *Lorna Foss*. (Above, courtesy Washington State Historical Society; below, UW Libraries, Special Collections, No. 7604.)

WHITE-HULLED *WANDERER*. The widely known steam tug *Wanderer* is shown here with her hull painted white, the paint scheme used when she was operated by the Foss Company in Seattle in the late 1930s and early 1940s. For 20 years, from 1916 until 1936, the stately workboat was owned by Merrill and Ring Lumber Company and towed log rafts, from the Pysht River on the Strait of Juan de Fuca to Port Angeles and Puget Sound ports, before she was purchased by Foss in 1936. (Courtesy PSMHS, No. 2678-8.)

TUGS AND THE COMMUNITY. Puget Sound tugboat companies large and small have a long tradition of involvement in their communities. Here several Foss tugs, their crews, and guests participate in a water carnival held at Point Defiance in Tacoma in 1938. Sponsored by the city's Young Men's Business Club, the event included a tugboat race, family rowboats, yachts, and commercial fishing boats in addition to tugs. The event attracted an estimated 25,000 people. (Courtesy Tacoma Public Library, No. D7207-13.)

FIREFIGHTING TUGBOATS. Four Foss tugs are shown in 1935 fighting a warehouse fire on the Tacoma waterfront. Pouring water from their powerful fire monitor nozzles on the fire in the Waterside Milling Company warehouse at the Old London Dock are, from left to right, the *Foss No. 12*, *Justine Foss*, *Henrietta Foss*, and *Foss No. 17*. Working with local fireboats and shoreside fire trucks, monitor-equipped tugs based at Puget Sound ports helped combat waterfront fires and prevented loss of property and life. (Courtesy Tacoma Public Library.)

BURNING TUG. In addition to some tugboats helping fight fires, many were themselves burned. Built in 1879 as a lighthouse tender (later converted to the steam tugboat *Daniel Kern*), the tug was scrapped and burned in 1939 at Richmond Beach north of Seattle. Other old, unused tugs and also sailing ships were set afire as part of various community holidays and other events held throughout the Sound. (Courtesy MOHAI, No. PI-25950.)

Three

A Tugboat Family's Story 1915–2008

When V. C. "Cap" Webster established Seattle's Fremont Towing Company in 1915, he could not have envisioned that his fledgling tugboat business would still be operating more than 90 years later. But through a combination of sea smarts, customer service, and hard work, the renamed Fremont Tugboat Company has become a small but legendary part of Puget Sound tugboat history.

Evolving together with Cap Webster's original Fremont Boat Market brokerage business, the tugboat side expanded when O. H. "Doc" bought both enterprises in 1928. Under Doc's leadership, the companies survived the major economic depression of 1929 and continued their growth during and following World War II. However, it was not until Doc's son Mark Freeman completed his U.S. Coast Guard active duty in 1959 that the tugboat business took off. From his teenage days retrieving stray logs for lumber companies with a series of small tugs, Mark's maritime life gravitated toward tugboats.

Purchasing, refitting, and operating a changing fleet of small- and medium-sized tugs, he stayed flexible, providing customized towing services on Lake Union as well as elsewhere on Puget Sound. In 2008, Mark and Margie Freeman operate and manage the Fremont Boat Company marina and son Erik and business partner Tom Bulson own Fremont Tugboat Company. It is a tugboat family story—one mirrored in the histories of other entrepreneurial Puget Sound marine towing businesses large and small.

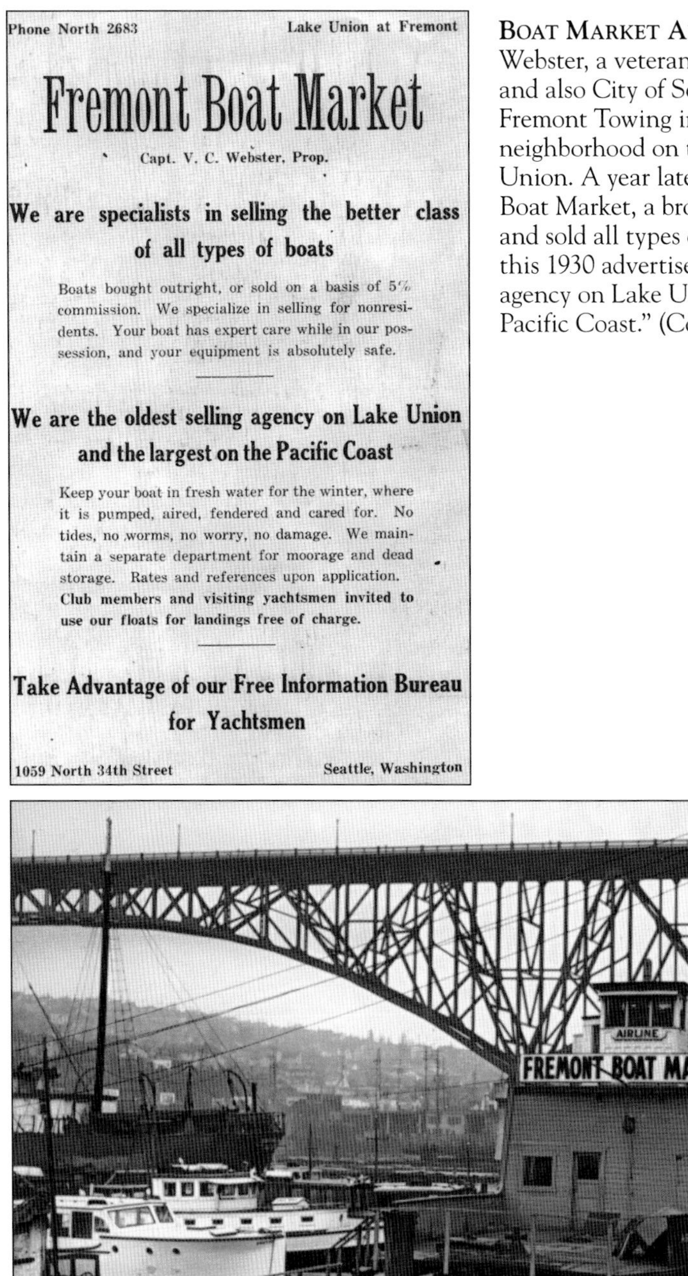

BOAT MARKET ADVERTISEMENT. V. C. "Cap" Webster, a veteran tugboat owner and skipper and also City of Seattle councilman, started Fremont Towing in 1915 in the Fremont neighborhood on the north side of Lake Union. A year later he established the Fremont Boat Market, a brokerage that built, bought, and sold all types of boats and as claimed in this 1930 advertisement was the "oldest-selling agency on Lake Union and the largest on the Pacific Coast." (Courtesy Mark Freeman.)

FERRYBOAT OFFICE. O. H. "Doc" Freeman bought the Fremont Boat Market business in 1928, rented moorage, and continued buying and selling boats as well as building and towing them. Doc bought property adjoining the boat market in 1938 and later brought in the old Puget Sound ferryboat *Airline,* which served as a floating office, shop, and family home. At the beginning of World War II in 1942, the ferry was taken over by the U.S. Coast Guard and used as a barracks ship. (Courtesy Mark Freeman.)

Boat Business Owner. A 27-year-old Doc Freeman is shown in this portrait wearing his familiar captain's hat. He had been the manager of "Cap" Webster's boat brokerage, handled day-to-day activities before he purchased it, and had learned the business from the bottom up. (Courtesy Mark Freeman.)

Tomorrow's Tugboat Captain. Taken in 1942, an eight-year-old Mark Freeman sits on the tow bitt of the tug *Skookum* in front of the Fremont Boat Market office aboard the former ferry *Airline*. The *Skookum* was sold to new owners in Portland, and it made a safe trip into the Pacific Ocean and down the Washington Coast to its new homeport. (Courtesy Mark Freeman.)

Family Business. The Freeman family (left) combined both business and home life at their north Lake Union waterfront site. In this 1947 photograph, Mark holds the family cat and from left to right are his mother May, sister Merry, and Doc outside the Freeman and Gibson chandlery located next to a renamed Fremont Boat Company. The same year, a new shoreside family home (below, under construction) was built over the marine hardware store was and operated by Doc and his partner, Russ Gibson. Through the years the building has been enlarged five times; the chandlery moved to a new location in 1999. Today the structure has become the O. H. Doc Freeman office building and also houses the offices of the Fremont Boat and Fremont Tugboat Companies. (Both courtesy Mark Freeman.)

FIRST TUGBOAT. In this 1949 photograph, Mark is shown shifting logs with a pike pole aboard his first tugboat, the *Seal Rock*. The boat was a round-bilge former U.S. Navy dory used aboard destroyers that he and his dad bought in surplus after World War II for $99. Mark used her to salvage stray logs off beaches to sell and for light towing. (Courtesy Mark Freeman.)

***JERKMORE* ON THE JOB.** The 36-foot-long *Jerkmore* was Mark's second tug and is shown here in 1954 salvaging logs in the Bainbridge Island's Rolling Bay area in western Puget Sound. During a heavy wind, the wayward logs had rolled out of a raft being towed by the *Western Star*, owned by Mark's brother-in-law Pat Stoppleman. The *Jerkmore*, named by Mark to describe its primary task, was converted from a surplus, diesel-powered U.S. Navy landing barge. (Courtesy Mark Freeman.)

COAST GUARD DAYS. This 1958 aerial photograph (above) shows Mark as the U.S. Coast Guard skipper of a 40-foot-long patrol and rescue boat operating out of the Grays Harbor Lifeboat Station in Westport, Washington. He joined the U.S. Coast Guard in March 1955, and after basic training served his four-year active duty tour on the Washington coast. Attaining the rank of 2nd Class Boatswain's Mate in 1957 (left), Mark was later awarded the U.S. Coast Guard Commendation Medal with Operational Distinguishing Device for his rescue of the crew of the former Liberty Ship *Sea Gate*. He saved 37 lives while on active duty. (Both courtesy of Mark Freeman.)

DOC AT WORK. In 1960, when this photograph was taken, Doc Freeman was 57 years old and busy managing his successful maritime businesses—buying and selling boats, ships, and marine equipment as well as waterfront properties. According to Mark, his dad "loved everything that had to do with the marine field." Freeman's very active, full maritime and family life ended when he passed away at the age of 60. (Courtesy Mark Freeman.)

STOKIN' ALONG. The 30-foot-long Fremont tug *Stoker* is shown underway in 1969 after being repowered with a new 150-horsepower diesel engine. Grandy Boat Company of Seattle built three of these boats for the government during World War II, and Mark purchased the *Stoker* from his dad's estate in 1963. (Courtesy Mark Freeman.)

MANILA UNDERWAY. In the years following Doc's death, Mark bought several tugs to expand the towing operations. Among them was the 45-foot-long tug *Manila* that was purchased in Everett. Originally bought for fun, it was soon put to work moving barges in Lake Union, in general towing, and shifting log rafts. She was sold in 1973 and was subsequently lost when she went aground in the Strait of Juan de Fuca. (Courtesy Mark Freeman.)

TUGS TINY AND TOUGH. With his tug *A-1* in the background, Mark stands in what was probably one of the tiniest working tugs in Puget Sound, the 15-foot-long *Barf.* Built in 1967 by the late master boatbuilder Al Glaser, the miniscule boat was for many years a familiar sight in Lake Union and also Olympia where she participated in the Harbor Days tugboat races. One of *Barf's* uses for 33 years before she was retired in 2000 was as a commuter boat carrying Mark and his wife, Margie, between their office and their houseboat across the Ship Canal. (Courtesy Mark Freeman.)

A-1 Condition. Moored in front of his and Margie's houseboat, Mark's 45-foot-long tug *A-1* operated under the Fremont Tugboat Company flag until 1994. Purchased in 1980, and restored and repowered, according to Mark she performed well as both a good tugboat and also as his and Margie's cruising boat. Elegant inside with a brass control panel and steering wheel, *A-1* was also fast and raced several times during the Olympia Harbor Days tugboat festival. (Courtesy Mark Freeman.)

Racing Tugs. The Fremont tug *Sovereign* is shown with the *Merilyn*, the former *Iver Foss*, during the 1985 Harbor Days tugboat races. *Sovereign* also won the Seattle races that same year. The 65-foot-long *Sovereign* was built in Sacramento, California, in 1941 and had been repowered with four 165-horsepower diesels when Mark bought her in 1984 to handle towing assignments for Seattle's growing crab boat fleet. (Courtesy Mark Freeman.)

Mighty Mite Tug. Mark is shown above at the helm of a former 20-foot ocean-fish seine skiff, which he converted into the tug *Stinger*. With her 14-foot beam or width, the short, squat "seine tug" is equipped with a 250-horsepower diesel engine and 38-inch, four-blade propeller. As shown below, this gives her the power and maneuverability to help shift fishing, processing, and other boats up to 250 feet long, as well as barges and houseboats, and handle other assignments in Lake Union. The *Stinger* was chartered in 2005 and 2006 by Foss Maritime for an oil refinery construction project in the Russian Far East, and in Puget Sound she accompanies Fremont's tug *Dixie* on all large vessel towing jobs. (Both courtesy Mark Freeman.)

TOWING TWOSOME. Fremont Tugboat Company handles varied towing assignments on Lake Union and elsewhere in Puget Sound and is now owned and operated by Mark's son Erik and his business partner Tom Bulson. Shown above, the 45-foot-long, 380-horsepower *Standfast* tows the 120-foot-long Foss Maritime customer hospitality yacht *Thea Foss*, built in 1930 for the late movie actor John Barrymore, through the ship canal between Ballard and Lake Union. The photograph below shows the *Standfast* and the *Spitfire* moving the U.S. Navy Reserve minesweeper USS *Pledge*, built in 1955 in Tacoma by J. M. Martinac Shipbuilding, away from Lake Union Dry Dock after a maintenance dry dock haul out. (Both courtesy Mark Freeman.)

Tugboat Transition. A tugboat transition took place at Fremont Tugboat Company in 2006 when the *Sovereign* was retired and sold, and its replacement *Dixie* took over as the lead tug for shifting large fishing vessels and barges. The *Dixie* was built for towing on Lake Roosevelt in eastern Washington, moved to the Columbia River, and then Alaska. Purchased by Fremont Tugboat Company, it was refitted and placed in service on Lake Union and Puget Sound. (Courtesy Mark Freeman.)

Coast Guard Assist. A historically appropriate event took place in 1994 when two U.S. Coast Guard vessels, one on active duty and the other retired, met on Lake Union. The 65-foot-long Fremont tug *Blueberry* is shown moving the 210-foot-long U.S. Coast Guard cutter *Alert* at Lake Union Dry Dock. Owned by U.S. Coast Guard veteran Mark Freeman since 1994, the former U.S. Coast Guard buoy tender and tug *Blueberry* was built in Tacoma in 1941 and decommissioned and sold as surplus in 1976. (Courtesy Mark Freeman.)

Steam Crane Shift. Fremont's 50-foot-long tug *Dixie* is shown here towing the *Foss 300* steam crane barge back to its moorage at the Foss Maritime headquarters and shipyard near Ballard. The 75-ton-capacity, steam engine–powered crane was built in 1943 and has had many common and some unusual assignments through the years, including salvaging a sunken airliner that crashed into Puget Sound shortly after takeoff in 1956. (Courtesy Mark Freeman.)

Towing Twins. A veteran Fremont tug, the World War II–era *Standfast* at right has been working hard since purchased in 1972 and is seen here together with the company's newest tug acquisition, the 42-foot-long *Grace*. The *Grace* is the former *Grace Foss* built in 1968 in Anacortes at Pacific Shipyards, and Mark Freeman bought her from Foss in 2005. The tug was ready for service after going through a haul out and major refit in 2008. (Courtesy Mark Freeman.)

FREMONT CAPTAINS AND CREW. The Fremont Boat Company and Fremont Tugboat Company core crew are shown above aboard the tugboat *Grace*. From left to right are Margie Freeman, Capt. Mark Freeman, Capt. Erik Freeman, Keegan Brown, Capt. Tom Bulson, and chief engineer Adair James. Erik and Tom bought the tug company from Mark in 1995, continuing three generations of ownership within the Freeman family. The Fremont Tugboat Company, established in 1915, has a more than 90-year Lake Union and Puget Sound towing history. Mark and Margie continue to own and operate Fremont Boat Company on Lake Union, which includes the 120-slip marina moorage. In the photograph at left, Mark Freeman stands at the rail of his buoy tender and tug *Blueberry* prior to her escort of the U.S. Coast Guard training square-rigger *Eagle* into Seattle in early July 2008. (Above, courtesy Karla Fowler; at left, Chuck Fowler.)

Four

War, Renewal, and New Business 1941–1979

While in a political context, world wars and other international conflicts are unfortunate occurrences, they nonetheless spur technological innovation and economic growth. This was the case during World War II as the United States geared up to meet the threats of its enemies in Europe and Asia. And along with building up arms production, tugboats and worldwide towing services became an essential part of the war effort.

Commercial tugs were chartered by the government, new construction streamlined, and other improvements were implemented. These developments, hundreds of surplus tugboats and trained crews, helped the civilian industry grow after the war and into the following decades. However, this almost 40-year-long era also produced new tug designs and marine towing innovations. Also, markets expanded to Alaska during the late 1960s and 1970s after vast new oil fields were discovered and also to Pacific Rim nations as their revitalized economies developed.

In addition, many tug company buyouts, consolidations, and mergers accelerated as the industry reflected national economic trends and business organization patterns, including the creation of corporate conglomerates. But rough, uncertain seas in the tugboat business during this period presaged calmer times ahead. For more than a century, the Puget Sound towing industry had weathered shifting storms, and it was now poised for an exciting new era of innovation and expansion.

FIREFIGHTING TUG. In wartime gray paint, the *Foss No. 18*, formerly the tugboat *Alice*, is seen testing firefighting equipment in Seattle in 1942. Many Puget Sound tugboats chartered by the government during World War II, assigned to the U.S. Army Transportation Service, were used for various wartime support operations in Puget Sound, Alaska, and throughout the Pacific. (Courtesy Foss Maritime.)

MILITARY MIKIMIKI. Designed by L. H. (Leigh Hill) Coolidge of Seattle in the late 1920s, sixty-nine wooden tugs of the "Mikimiki" class were built at shipyards throughout the nation for World War II support operations. The U.S. Army tug *LT 160*, shown here, was built and launched in 1944 by Northwestern Shipyard in Bellingham. Sold as surplus after the war, she became the *Martha Foss* in 1951. (Courtesy Mark Freeman.)

Civilian Conversion. The 125-foot-long tug *Monarch,* shown here in 1949, was a single screw propeller "Miki" tug that served during the war as the *LT 466.* Powered by a 1,200-horsepower diesel engine, she was purchased and operated by Puget Sound Tug and Barge Company until retired and scuttled in 1980. The first tug built of this design in the 1930s, for a Hawaiian tug company, was called the *Mikimiki,* which means "on time." Mikimikis were twin screw tugs and Mikis were single screw. (Courtesy Mark Freeman.)

Tug Haulout. The deep, heavy-hull design of a Miki tug is shown in this 1947 photograph of the *Justine Foss* hauled out for maintenance at Todd Pacific shipyard in Seattle. The former U.S. Army *LT-378,* the 117-foot-long tug was built at the Barbee Marine Yard near Renton in 1944, declared surplus in 1946 after World War II, and purchased by Foss. The *Justine* had an enviable towing career, including Alaska and Hawaii assignments, until retired from active Foss service in 1971. (Courtesy Foss Maritime.)

MULTITASK TUG. The 43-foot-long tug *Joe Foss* was a multitasking tugboat as part of the Foss Tacoma fleet. Ship assisting, barge shifting and towing, log towing, and even firefighting, the *Joe* did it all. Shown above alongside the log ship *Fusan Maru* in the 1960s, the tug was built in the Foss shipyard in Tacoma in 1942 and served actively in Commencement Bay for 30 years. Among the *Joe's* more unusual assignments, as seen below, was the 1943 move of the Foss floating office building from its historical Dock Street site on the Tacoma waterfront to its F Street location on the tide flats. (Both courtesy Foss Maritime.)

TOWING TALK. Crewmembers from the tugboats *Iver Foss* and *Foss No. 21* and a cargo schooner apparently talk over a tow before the operation in this 1930s photograph. The 65-foot-long *Iver* was designed by L. H. Coolidge and built in Port Angeles in 1925 for the Angeles Gravel and Supply Yard and named *Angeles*. The tug was acquired in 1926 by Foss, who used it to start the company's Port Angeles division; she worked 47 years before her retirement. The *Foss No. 21*, formerly the *Fearless*, was built in 1900 for the Tacoma Tug and Barge Company. Purchased by Foss in 1925, she worked for 41 years under the Foss flag, mainly in Port Angeles but also along the Washington coast and in Puget Sound. She was later purchased by the Western Tugboat Company, which changed her name back to the original *Fearless*. (Courtesy Foss Maritime.)

WANDERING TOW. Following an early log and sailing ship towing career in the late 1890s and the early part of the 1900s, the famed steam tug *Wanderer* also towed railroad car barges as shown here during the mid-1940s. Railroad barge towing became the venerable tug's primary assignment during the next decade, moving railcars between Seattle, Port Townsend, and Bellingham. However, even before this period the famous, now historic and still steam-powered tugboat began to show the wooden tug wounds accumulated over a half century of towing. As recounted in his book, *Foss: Ninety Years of Towboating*, Foss Maritime historian Mike Skalley noted that even in the late 1930s "her timbers were becoming slack in the joints" and her crew reported that the "bilge pumps ran continually to take care of the leaks." (Courtesy PSMHS, No. 2678-10.)

End of the Tow Line. The final days of the *Wanderer* came in February 1947. As shown here, strong currents and a heavy fog caused her to run aground off Double Bluff on the southwest side of Whidbey Island. Although the hull was not opened up or severely damaged, the legendary tug was obsolete; no longer seaworthy, she was subsequently stripped, towed to the Nisqually River flats, beached, and made part of a breakwater. (Courtesy PSMHS, No. 2678-17.)

Glory Days. This dramatic painting by Pacific Northwest marine artist Steve Mayo shows the *Wanderer* in heavy seas under a threatening sky in the Strait of Juan de Fuca when she was part of the Puget Sound Tugboat Company fleet from 1890 until 1916. The tug was later sold to Merrill and Ring Lumber Company, and she towed log rafts to lumber mills for the next 20 years before being sold to Foss Launch and Tug Company in 1936. (Courtesy Steve Mayo.)

SMALLER TUG FLEETS. Many smaller tugboat companies outside of the Seattle and Tacoma areas also had relatively large tugboat fleets. The American Tugboat Company of Everett tied 19 of their tugs together for the impressive group photograph above, taken in the 1940s. The American fleet included the *Mary D. Hume*, *Irene*, *Elmore*, *Tillicum*, and the *Manila* and provided towing services in Puget Sound, Canada, and Alaska. Gilkey Brothers Towing Company also had a varied fleet based in Anacortes on the Guemes Channel. Shown in the photograph below are, from left to right, (foreground) the *Hioma* and *Governor*; (background) *Sound*, *Intrepid*, *Columbia*, *Bahada*, and *Sea King*. In 1941, Gilkey and Pacific Towboat merged under the Pacific Towboat name with Gilkey handling Anacortes operations and Pacific Towboat handling the Everett business. The merged business later became part of Foss. (Both courtesy Mark Freeman.)

TYEE—ACT TWO. After its many years as part of the Puget Sound Tugboat Company, the renowned steam tug *Tyee* was sold to Cary-Davis Towing and later to Bellingham Tug and Barge Company. In the center of the photograph above, she is shown moored with other company tugs, the *Intrepid* on the *Tyee's* port or left side and on the right the *Automatic* and the *Shamrock II*. The graceful, more than 140-foot-long shear line of the *Tyee's* hull is revealed in the photograph below, taken on the Bellingham waterfront around 1924. The Bellingham Tug and Barge Company was sold to Foss in 1949. (Both courtesy Mark Freeman.)

TACOMA TUG. Several Puget Sound tugboats through the years have carried the name *Favorite*, beginning with the huge side-wheel steamer that operated in north Sound waters from 1869 until 1921. A much smaller version, at 35 feet in length, was built by Mojean and Erickson boatbuilders in 1937 and towed logs and barges in Commencement Bay for the Tacoma Tug and Barge Company through the 1940s and the 1950s. (Courtesy PSMHS.)

RELIANCE RACING. The 41-foot-long tug *Reliance* won Olympia Harbor Days tugboat races in 1980 and 1981 when owned by veteran master Phil Shiveley, but she also had a long working career. Built in Willapa Harbor in 1909 for the E. E. Case Logging Company, the tug was a log patrol boat and camp tender on the Washington coast. *Reliance* was purchased in 1976, restored, and put into operation in Puget Sound by the Shiveley Tugboat Company of Bainbridge Island. (Courtesy Scott Schoch.)

HEAD-ON FAVORITE. This dramatic bow-on painting by Karla Fowler of the small tugboat *Favorite* depicts her pushing water during the 1983 Olympia Harbor Days tugboat race. Owned at the time by Phil Martin, the tug was homeported in Friday Harbor and was used to tow barges and for other light towing work. The painting was purchased by the late maritime historian, collector, and curator Bill Somers for the outstanding collection in his Museum of Puget Sound on Stretch Island in Graperview. Throughout his long life, Somers accumulated the finest collection of Puget Sound Mosquito Fleet artifacts to be seen anywhere. (Courtesy Karla Fowler.)

ELMORE PAST. The tugboat *Elmore* has an extensive history on the Columbia River and in Puget Sound. Built as the steam cannery tender, the *R. P. Elmore* was constructed in 1890 for the Elmore Packing Company of Astoria, Oregon. The tug was purchased in 1898 by the then newly formed American Tugboat Company of Everett as the first tug in its fleet. Her name was changed to simply *Elmore* in 1923, and she was repowered with a 110-horsepower Washington Iron Works diesel engine. The photograph above shows her in 1941 in Seattle taking a tow past the Phoenix Mill in the background and under the Ballard Bridge. The tranquil 1950 photograph below shows her next to a purse seine fish boat in Burrows Bay in the Rosario Strait in north Puget Sound. (Both courtesy Mark Freeman.)

Elmore Present. After more than a century, the long-lived *Elmore* continues to ply the waters of Puget Sound—but today for recreational cruising. Under owners Dee and Sarah Meek, she participated in Harbor Days events and tug races (above) and also International Retired Tugboat Association tug meet gatherings. After five diesel engine changes during more than 80 years, in 2008, the fully restored *Elmore* was operating with her 110-horsepower Atlas Imperial engine (below). Even as a recreational tug, the *Elmore*'s operating costs have increased a bit since she was a steamer. Her ledger sheet for December 1904 reveals that the steam engine boiler cost $177 to generate and her crew payroll totaled $410. (Above, courtesy Karla Fowler; below, Mark Freeman.)

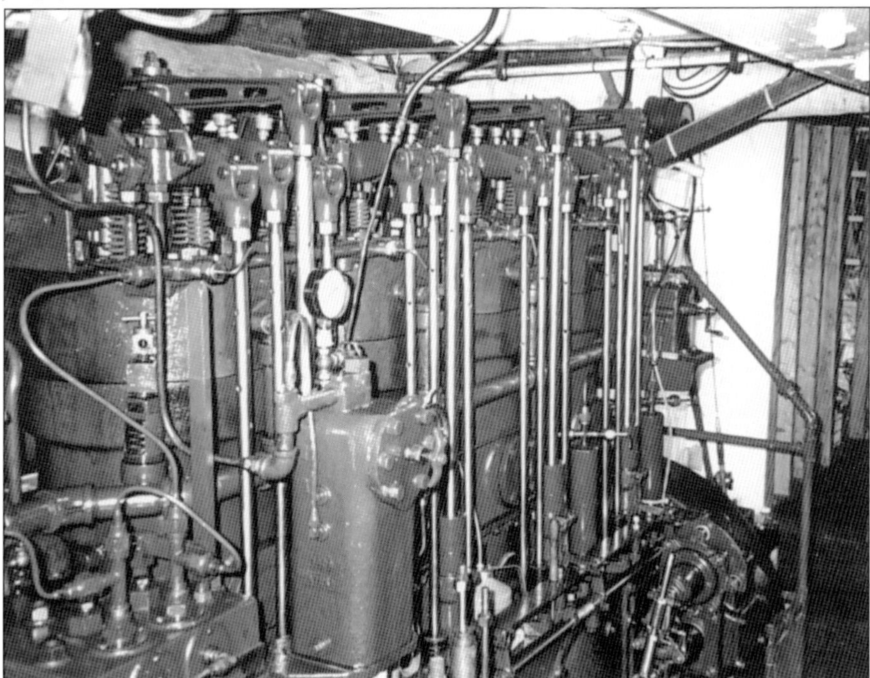

Tugboat Evolution. The former tug *Alice*, built in 1892, continued to evolve during the 1940s. The process began in 1905 when the former steam cannery tender was converted to a tugboat by the Crosby Towboat Company of Seattle. Merging with the Chesley Towboat Company in 1912, the business and the *Alice* were purchased by Foss Launch and Tug Company in 1919 and renamed the *Foss No. 18*. After two decades of service as one of the hardest working, most efficient tugs in the Sound, she was hauled out for a major rebuild in 1940; stripped down to her frame and most of the planking removed for replacement. A new 450-horsepower Enterprise diesel engine was also installed and the almost half-century-old tug was ready for many more years of profitable towing. The photograph below, taken from an annual Foss calendar in the 1950s, shows the *Foss No. 18* with a bow wave "bone in her teeth," ready to go to work. (Both courtesy Foss Maritime.)

Chris Crossing Time. The 51-foot-long *Chris Foss* shown in the photograph above was built in 1925 at the Sieverson Shipyard in Seattle for Wagner Towboat Company and was originally named *Crest*. Foss Launch and Tug Company purchased her along with the Wagner business in 1937, and the *Crest* was renamed. Designed by L. H Coolidge, who also designed the famous Mikimiki tugs, the *Chris Foss* had made salmon cannery barge tows to and from Alaska before becoming part of the Foss fleet. After almost a decade of towing for Foss, the *Chris* grounded on the Dungeness Spit at Port Angeles in 1946 while towing a barge. Subsequently, the company decided to retire her, and she was sold and refitted and continued working for another decade under her new owners. The photograph below shows the well-worn tug under tow in 1956 after she was sold to Doc Freeman for resale. (Above, courtesy Foss Maritime; below, Mark Freeman.)

Empowering Engines. Diesel engines built by Washington Iron Works in Seattle powered many tugboats, fish boats, and other vessels on Puget Sound and were widely known for their ruggedness and reliability. Shown above is an eight-cylinder Washington heavy-duty marine engine generally similar to the six-cylinder 700-horsepower engine in the famous tugboat *Arthur Foss* shown below. The 110-foot-long *Arthur*, built in 1889 on the Columbia River in Oregon as the *Wallowa*, had a long and distinguished towing career. She was purchased by Foss Launch and Tug Company in 1929 and served in Alaska, later in the Pacific during World War II, and in Puget Sound until 1968. (Both courtesy Mark Freeman.)

DOMINATING DIESELS. As shown in the photograph at right of a late 1940s Washington Iron Works promotional booklet, the company offered a full range of heavy-duty diesel engines for marine, power generation, and other applications. From 90 to 850 horsepower, Washington diesels were highly regarded by tugboat owners as well as tug skippers for their compatibility with many hull types and propulsion systems. The photograph below shows the size of just one of the engine's eight pistons in comparison to the mechanic working on it. One of the advantages of Washington diesels was the accessibility to pistons and other internal parts through large side access panels. (Both courtesy Mark Freeman.)

Construction Tug. In addition to tugboats owned by strictly towing businesses, marine construction companies also operated tugs to move pile drivers, barges, and other heavy equipment throughout Puget Sound. A pioneer in this field is Manson Construction Company of Seattle. Founded by Swedish immigrant Peter Manson in 1905, the *Peter* M was among the company's many tugboats. The tug, built in 1950, supported many waterfront projects including moving pile drivers for the construction and maintenance of ferry docks such as at the Lofall terminal on Hood Canal shown in the photograph above. The *Peter* M. is shown below in the Duwamish River in Seattle towing an equipment barge loaded with poles for a pile-driving project. (Both courtesy Manson Construction Company.)

TOW BRIDGE. Among the more historically interesting, but also somewhat sad, tugboat projects are the tows of old ships from "mothball" or reserve fleet moorages to shipyards to be scrapped. Here the former U.S. Army transport ship *Republic*, built in 1907, is towed under the Tacoma Narrows Bridge by the *Agnes Foss* and *Donna Foss* in 1952 on her way to being dismantled for her scrap-metal value. (Courtesy PSMHS.)

CRASH RECOVERY. The *Foss No. 18* is shown alongside the *Foss 300* steam-crane barge during the 1956 recovery of a Northwest Airlines airliner that ditched in Puget Sound shortly after takeoff from Seattle-Tacoma International Airport. Thirty-eight passengers were rescued and assisted by the crews of two U.S. Air Force seaplanes, U.S. Coast Guard cutter *CG-83527*, and tugboats that responded to the accident; however, five onboard were lost. (Courtesy Foss Maritime.)

TUGBOAT CAPTAIN. Capt. Ray Quinn, shown here in 1938 aboard the well-regarded tugboat *Neptune* when he was her master, had a long and distinguished maritime career. As related by Ron Burke, editor of the Puget Sound Maritime Historical Society journal *Sea Chest*, Ray started his career when he was 16 years old as a deckhand on the two-man tug *Christy R.* of the Cary-Davis Tug and Barge Company. At 17 he was the mate or second in command of the famous tug *Equator* and at 18 was its captain. Quinn was then captain of the *Dolly C.*, *Douglas*, *Goliah*, and *Neptune*. Switching to Foss, he was master of the *Anna Foss* and the well-known *Wanderer*, according to Burke. During World War II he was active as a tugboat captain and also chief mate of a Victory ship. Returning to Foss after the war, he was master of the *Agnes Foss* when it towed the surplus transport *Republic* from Puget Sound to the Panama Canal en route to scrapping. In 1954, the experienced, well-traveled captain ended his long career by becoming a Puget Sound pilot, a role in which he served for 20 years before his retirement. (Courtesy PSMHS.)

NEPTUNE AND CREW. The captain and crew of any tugboat were key elements in its professional, practical, and profitable operation. Shown above in the late 1930s is the crew of the *Neptune*, one of the legendary tugs of Puget Sound and the flagship of the Puget Sound Tug and Barge fleet. Built in 1904 as the U.S. Public Health Service passenger steamer *R. M. Woodward*, the *Neptune* was purchased by Puget Sound Tug in San Francisco in 1937. She was towed to the Sound and refitted with a 1,050-horsepower Fairbanks diesel engine and had a long, successful towing career. As seen underway on the Seattle waterfront in the photograph below, the *Neptune* combined masterful workboat design and pure power. During a 1939 tugboat race in Seattle, her top speed was almost 16 knots and she averaged more than 13 knots. (Both courtesy PSMHS; above No. 1698-15, below No. 1698-14.)

CALM AND ROUGH CONDITIONS. The *Neptune* performed well in both calm and rough seas as shown in these images. The photograph above, taken in the late mid-1940s, shows the legendary tug leaving a deep trough of water along the port (left side) of her hull with the Seattle skyline in the background. Before entering Puget Sound Tug and Barge service in 1937, she was rebuilt to plans created by the well-known naval architect H. C. Hanson, who during his career designed many noted vessels including tugs. The photograph below shows the *Neptune* running in "sloppy" weather in the Sound, looking partially submerged but because of her hefty, buoyant hull, is in no risk. (Both courtesy PSMHS; above No. 1698-34, below No. 1968-31.)

TOWERING TOW. The *Neptune* is shown in the early 1940s towing the big Alaska cannery transport ship *Otsego* from Puget Sound on her way through the Ballard Locks and into Lake Union to tie up at the Libby, McNeil, and Libby Company dock. In August 1946, the *Neptune* was turned over to Foss Launch and Tug Company as part of a court settlement over the distribution of profits from World War II towing contracts. She was renamed *Wedell Foss* and, during the next 30 years at Foss, made an enviable record towing barges, primarily carrying railcars but also wood pulp and chips, oil, chemicals, and similar products. (Courtesy PSMHS, No. 1698-19.)

SUBMARINE AND FERRY BOAT. The submarine USS *Puffer*, used for training at the U.S. Naval Reserve Center at south Lake Union between 1947 and 1960, is shown above being towed through the Fremont Bridge in Seattle by the Puget Sound Tug and Barge Company's second tug *Neptune* at the sub's stern and the *Trojan* on the bow. The ocean tow in 1960 took the submarine to a Portland, Oregon, shipyard for scrapping. In the 1950s photograph below, the Puget Sound Tug and Barge tug *Goliah* is shown alongside the Washington State ferry *Chippewa* at Colman Dock terminal in Seattle. The *Goliah* of this period was the third to bear the famous name. (Both courtesy MOHAI; above No. 1986.5.13972.1, below No. 1986.5.13225.3.)

TRADITIONAL TUGS. Two longtime traditionally designed tugs of the early Foss fleet are shown here in different towing and weather conditions. The 63-foot-long *Lorna Foss*, built in Hoquiam in 1903, is depicted above in the 1940s towing a long log raft through the Montlake Cut into Lake Washington. Retired by Foss in 1957, the tug has been restored, maintained, and operated by Dan Grinstead. Seen below is the 53-foot-long *Drew Foss*, named for the son of Henry and Agnes, which was built at the Foss Tacoma shipyard in 1929 and was retired in 1975 after a more than four-decade-long career. (Above, courtesy UW Libraries, Special Collections, No. UW25805; below, PSMHS.)

NEXT GENERATION TUGS. With many of the pre–World War II wooden tugs beginning to reach their maximum service age, Foss Launch and Tug Company began building a new generation of tugboats in the late 1950s. The first of these were the *Carol Foss* and *Shannon Foss*, 84-foot-long steel tugs that were each equipped initially with a 1,200-horsepower diesel engine. The photograph at left shows a heavy-capacity floating crane launching the *Carol Foss* at the Todd Shipyard where she and the *Shannon* were built in 1957. Following launch, the *Carol* was towed to the Foss Seattle shipyard where her diesel engine was installed and fitting out was completed. In the photograph below, the *Shannon Foss* is shown in the foreground running with her sister tug *Carol*. (Both courtesy Foss Maritime.)

PULLING POWER. This striking image of the *Carol Foss* underway shows the tug's towing and pulling power. The *Carol* and *Shannon* were the pride of the Foss Seattle harbor fleet until 1970 when the newer, more powerful *Shelley Foss* became the company's primary ship-assist tugboat on Elliott Bay. But the working career of the *Carol Foss* was not over. In 1977 after 19 years docking and undocking ships in Seattle as well as towing and helping set anchors during the construction of the Hood Canal Floating Bridge, the tug's initial power plant was replaced with a new 1,600-horsepower diesel engine. The timing of the *Carol's* repowering was good as newer, larger ships were calling on Seattle and both vessel and barge traffic was increasing. After long successful careers, the *Carol* and *Shannon* were retired from Foss service in the early 1990s, sold to new owners, and still working in 2008. (Courtesy Mark Freeman.)

BRAWNY *BEE*. The venerable tug *Bee*, built in 1901, was a well-known tugboat on Puget Sound for almost a century. First owned by the Everett Tug and Barge Company as the steam tug *Nellie Pearson*, according to maritime historian Karl House, in 1917 she was purchased by Washington Tug and Barge Company. The tug was rebuilt in 1921, repowered with a 100-horsepower diesel engine, and renamed *Bee*. She was active in Puget Sound during World War II and after the war did general towing work including that of oil barges. The *Bee* was sold and worked for Western Towboat from 1964 to 1972. Her next owner was Keith Sternberg, who installed a 130-horsepower Atlas diesel in her, which provided plenty of power to shift and tow logs throughout the Sound. Gary Duff then took over ownership of the *Bee* and did local towing until the historic tug was sold again and eventually went to Alaska. (Both courtesy Mark Freeman.)

TUG TASKS. Tugboats in Puget Sound and elsewhere take on varied and interesting tasks. In the photograph above, the 66-foot-long *David Foss* side tows the navy submarine USS *Bowfin* away from the U.S. Naval Reserve Center at south Lake Union in 1970. The *Bowfin* was the training submarine at the center from 1960 until 1970 when she was towed to Honolulu to become a permanent exhibit at the site of the USS *Arizona* Memorial at Pearl Harbor. Firefighting is another auxiliary but important tugboat assignment, and the *Josie Foss* and *Henrietta Foss* are shown below fighting a lumber mill blaze in Seattle's Ballard district in 1969. (Both courtesy MOHAI; above No. 1986.5.54716, below 5.51077.1.)

Tall Ship Assists. Two U.S. Navy YTL tugs assist the Danish Navy training square-rigger *Danmark* to her berth in the photograph above during a visit to Seattle in 1946. The imposing vessel was visiting the United States at the outbreak of World War II and Danish officials subsequently loaned the tall ship to the U.S. Coast Guard to train 5,000 future officers during the war. Following the end of hostilities, the *Danmark* was sent on a "thank you" cruise to U.S. ports and others including a stopover in Puget Sound. The photograph below shows the four-mast schooner yacht *Fantome* in the late 1940s being towed from Portage Bay through the open University Bridge by the *Adeline Foss*. The *Fantome*, owned by British brewing company magnate A. E. Guiness, was a familiar sight in Seattle until she left Puget Sound in 1953. (Above, courtesy UW Libraries, Special Collections; below, Mark Freeman.)

Tall Ships Too. The 75-foot-long tug *Phillips Foss* is seen above towing the cod fish schooner *Wawona* in Puget Sound in 1964. A National Historic Landmark vessel, the *Wawona* was the last survivor in 2008 of Puget Sound's once extensive lumber and fishing schooner fleet. The *Phillips* was built in 1916 and owned during World War II by Puget Sound Tug and Barge Company until she was acquired by Foss Launch and Tug Company in 1946 and served with Foss until she retired in 1967. With its bow to the Japanese training square-rigger *Kaiwo Maru I*, the photograph below shows the Puget Sound Tug and Barge tugboat *Goliah*, built during World War II, moving the tall ship to its berth in Seattle's Elliott Bay. The 307-foot-long, four-mast sailing ship visited Seattle in 1968 during one of its merchant marine cadet training voyages. (Above, courtesy Mark Freeman; below, Crowley Maritime.)

POWER TUGS. Three powerful tugs in the Puget Sound Tug and Barge fleet operated from Seattle in the 1960s and 1970s. Shown above on Elliott Bay, from front to back, are the *Retriever* and her sister tugs *Goliah* and *Restless*. All three tugs, powered by twin 635 diesel engines, were built during World War II and operated by the U.S. Army and Navy. With the construction in Alaska of the Distant Early Warning (DEW) line of radar stations during the 1950s and the discovery of oil in Alaska in the late 1960s, tug companies responded by developing long-distance barge towing operations to the North Pacific. The 1,600-horsepower *Vigorous*, another Puget Sound Tug company tugboat, is seen below in the early 1970s approaching a Hydro-Train barge loaded with railcars, vehicles, and other cargo bound for Alaska. (Above, courtesy Mark Freeman; below, Crowley Maritime.)

Ship Tugs. In addition to barge and other towing jobs, shifting and assisting ships in harbors is another key part of tugboat operations. The photograph above shows the Puget Sound Tug and Barge tug *Retriever* assisting the freighter *Japan Mail* in Seattle's Elliott Bay with the Space Needle in the background. In the photograph below, the 65-foot-long Puget Sound Tug and Barge tug *Trojan* moves the Amphibious Transport USS *Trenton, LPD14*, away from Lockheed Shipyard in Seattle following her launch in August 1968. The 65-foot-long *Trojan* was one of three former U.S. Navy tugs that were refitted with new wheelhouses and crew quarters as well as four tandem diesels totaling 800 horsepower. (Above, courtesy Mark Freeman; below, Crowley Maritime.)

FATHER AND SON TUGS. The Foss Maritime Company had a long tradition of naming their tugs after family members. Seen in the photograph above, the 149-foot-long, 5,000-horsepower tug *Henry Foss* was built in 1943 during World War II for the U.S. Army Transportation Service and was named for company founders Andrew and Thea Foss's youngest son. Shown below moored at the Foss corporate office in Seattle is the newest *Drew Foss*, the second tugboat to carry the name of the son of Henry and Agnes Foss. Built in Louisiana in 1977 by McDermott Shipbuilding, the 120-foot-long tug has towed in Alaska, the Caribbean, Atlantic Coast, South America, and even the Great Lakes during the past three decades. (Above, courtesy Foss Maritime; below, Mark Freeman.)

Five

The Modern Tugboat Era 1980–2008

Beginning in 1980s, exciting new design and propulsion developments emerged within the tugboat industry. More maneuverable, flexible tractor tugs heralded new approaches to ship escort and assist, towing, and related assignments. Coupled with cycloidal and Kort nozzle propulsion systems and Z-drives, these innovations quietly revolutionized tugboat operations on Puget Sound, elsewhere in the nation, and around the world.

Puget Sound and British Columbia–based naval architects and tugboat companies created design breakthroughs, such as the Foss Maritime Company with its first tractor tugs in the early 1980s. Other companies large and small developed their own innovations in both tugboat technology and towing applications.

Many Puget Sound tugboat companies began as small family businesses connected fully to their home communities. As these customer-focused enterprises evolved, they retained their family and community values in an era of rapid change. While hard at work on challenging assignments, tug company owners, crews, and shoreside support staffs continued to participate in popular local maritime events and contribute to their communities.

After more than 150 years of Puget Sound tugboating history, sea-smart competition still pervades the industry. However, the proud tradition of can-do cooperation and community service continues as well.

HISTORIC MANEUVERABILITY. In the early 1980s, Foss Maritime Company revolutionized tug design and technology when it built six new 100-foot-long "tractor" tugs for harbor ship assist work. Two historic eras are shown in the photograph above as the *Andrew Foss* moves the steam-powered, stern-wheel snagboat *W. T. Preston* during a tow to Anacortes in 1983 where the 163-foot-long steamer became an onshore museum exhibit vessel. The photograph below shows the total maneuverability of tractor tugs as the newest *Henry Foss* does a water "wheelie" by turning around in its own length. The tug's 3,000-horsepower diesel engine and vertical-bladed Voith-Schneider cycloidal propulsion system, which is mounted vertically mid-hull, provides outstanding maneuverability. (Both courtesy Foss Maritime.)

MILITARY TOWS. Through the years, Foss tractor tugs have taken on varied military towing assignments. In the photograph above, the tractor tug *Henry Foss* with the conventionally designed *Shelley Foss* alongside are shown assisting the 1,000-foot-long navy aircraft carrier USS *Constellation* to its berth in Seattle during a Fleet Week celebration in the mid-1970s. The photograph below shows the *Henry Foss* ready to assist the U.S. Coast Guard barque *Eagle* away from her berth on the Thea Foss Waterway at the end of the training square-rigger's 2008 visit during the Tall Ships Tacoma event on the Independence Day holiday on the Fourth of July weekend. The *Eagle*, based in New London, Connecticut, at the U.S. Coast Guard Academy, had thousands of onboard visitors during the five-day tall ships festival. (Above, courtesy Foss Maritime; below, Chuck Fowler.)

TUG FLEET LINEUP. One of the longtime traditions in the tugboat industry is the periodic lineup of a tug company's fleet for a group photograph used for promotional as well as historical documentation purposes. Eleven tugs of the Foss Maritime Company's Seattle-based harbor services fleet are shown rafted together in this 1986 photograph. Beginning with four tractor tugs, the lineup consists of, from left to right, the *Arthur Foss*; *Wedell Foss*; *Henry Foss*; and *Pacific Tractor*,

later renamed the *Brynn Foss*. Other tugs shown are the *Shelley Foss*, *Iver Foss*, *Catherine Foss*, *Diane Foss*, *Deborah Foss*, *Carol Foss*, and *Donna Foss*. At the time, the ages of the Foss tugboats in the photograph line up ranged from 1982, for the *Arthur Foss* and other tractor tugs, to 1958, for the *Carol Foss*. (Courtesy Foss Maritime.)

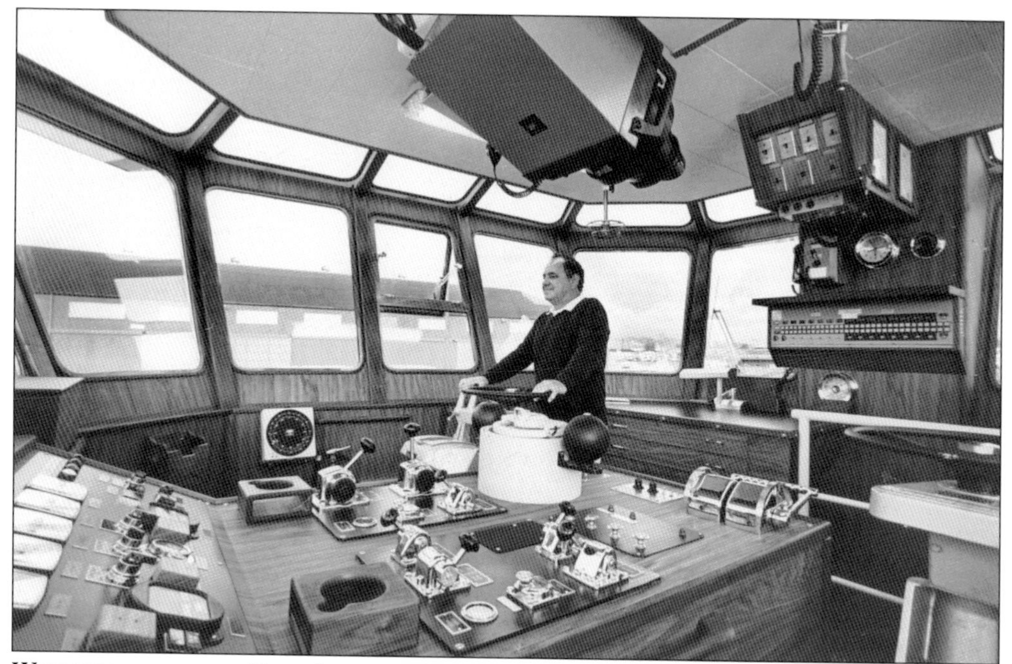

WHEELHOUSE WITH A VIEW. Longtime Foss tug captain Bill Shaffer is in the wheelhouse of the tractor tug *Henry Foss* in this 1982 photograph. According to company information, the tractor tug's window-enclosed wheelhouses were designed to allow maximum visibility of the deck and entire hull perimeter from the helm, or control position, to enhance work productivity and crew safety. (Courtesy Foss Maritime.)

AWESOME ASSIST. In this dramatic, creative photograph taken by the late Mike Stork, the tractor tug *Henry Foss* is shown assisting the container ship *Iwanuma Maru* in the Tacoma harbor with the bow of another massive ship looming above the water in the foreground at right. Mike, a career elementary school teacher, was the son of Foss captain Ed Stork and was a lifelong tug enthusiast, historian, and photographer. (Photograph by Mike Stork, courtesy Kathie Stork.)

GRACEFUL TUG. The 42-foot-long *Grace Foss* was built in 1968 by Pacific Shipyards in Anacortes primarily for towing and shifting logs and barges and other light work. She was one of nine steel harbor tugs built in the late 1960s that included *Joe Foss*, *Peggy Foss*, *Sam Foss*, *Omer Foss*, and *Lela Foss*. These small harbor tugs are known as "day boats" because their crews only work up to 12-hour shifts and do not need overnight crew quarters. (Courtesy Mark Freeman.)

BOEING BUILDING TOW. In 1980, the *Duncan Foss* moved the historic Boeing "Red Barn" building by barge up the Duwamish River in Seattle to its new site at the Museum of Flight at Boeing Field. The historic 1909 structure was Boeing's original manufacturing facility and now houses exhibits interpreting the early history of the company whose aircraft are known worldwide. (Courtesy Foss Maritime.)

TUG HARBOR SCENE. This active harbor scene on Tacoma's Commencement Bay in 1989 shows four Foss tugs providing barge towing as well as ship assist services. Shown at the top are two tractor tugs assisting a log ship; in the center is the *Claudia Foss* towing a gravel barge; and at bottom is the third *Iver Foss*, built in 1977, towing an oil-bunkering or ship-refueling barge. Tacoma was the original home of the business established in 1889 as the Foss Boathouse Company, later Foss Launch, followed by Foss Launch and Tug, Foss Dillingham, and today's Foss Maritime Company. This photograph was taken by Robin Paterson, owner, captain, and restorer of a series of retired tugboats through the years, including the original *Joe Foss* built in Tacoma in 1942. He was a longtime photographer of maritime scenes including tugboats and was a maritime historian and, more recently, an author. (Courtesy Robin Paterson.)

BIG TRACTOR TUG. Foss built two 155-foot-long, 8,000-horsepower, enhanced tractor tugboats, *Garth Foss* and *Lindsey Foss*, and they began escort and ship assist service in northern Puget Sound in 1994. The *Garth*, shown above underway in the Guemes Channel in Anacortes, is used primarily together with the *Lindsey* to escort and assist oil tankers from the Strait of Juan de Fuca to and from oil refineries at Anacortes and Ferndale near Bellingham. In the painting below by renowned marine artist Marshall Johnson, with Mount Rainier in the background, the *Garth* is shown assisting a Russian container ship at its berth at the Port of Tacoma. (Above, courtesy Mark Freeman; below, Marshall Johnson.)

HISTORIC OLYMPIA TUG. The historic Olympia tugboat *Sand Man* has been a south Puget Sound maritime icon for almost a century. Built by the Crawford and Reid shipyard in Tacoma in 1910, the venerable tug towed logs and gravel barges and did general towing work during its working years. Originally owned by and built for A. J. Weston, its later owners have included Delta V. Smyth, Franz Schlottmann, Bob Powell, and today the nonprofit Sand Man Foundation. *Sand Man* was selected in 1983 as the honored tugboat during the Olympia Harbor Days festival and appeared in the first in a series of marketing logos, shown above, that recognized the oldest tugs to participate. The dramatic photograph below by the late photographer Carl Cook shows the *Sand Man* at twilight underway on calm south Sound waters in the early 2000s. (Above, courtesy CM3 Associates; below, photograph by Carl Cook, courtesy Jadine Cook.)

HARBOR DAYS HIGHLIGHTS. The highlight of the Olympia Harbor Days festival, established in 1974 and presented annually on Labor Day weekend, is the tugboat races. Beginning historically in the late 1800s when tugs raced to be the first to tow square-rigged and other tall sailing ships to Puget Sound ports, tugboat racing on the Sound is a tradition more than a century old. Seattle's first races in the late 1930s were organized as part of a waterfront maritime event, but Olympia boasts the oldest-continuing series of races, which began in 1975. In the photograph below, the late Franz Schlottman, longtime owner, operator, and steward of the *Sand Man*, is seen in 1983 proudly holding his red captain's "logo" jacket, which featured his historic wooden tug. The 1989 Harbor Days promotional poster, shown at right, honored the tugboat *Elf* and recognized the 100th, or centennial, year of the Foss Maritime Company. (At right, courtesy CM3 Associates; below, Karla Fowler.)

Sand Man Restored. After an extensive six-year-long restoration process in Port Townsend and Olympia, the almost 100-year-old tugboat *Sand Man* returned in 2005 to her historic berth at Percival Landing in downtown Olympia. Donated to the nonprofit Sand Man Foundation in the late 1990s by then owner Bob Powell, money was raised through individual donations, government grants, and other contributions to fully restore the historic tug. She now serves a community, south Puget Sound, and as a regional maritime heritage icon and treasure. (Courtesy Chuck Fowler.)

ART AND ACTUALITY. The buoy tender and tug *Blueberry*, built in Tacoma at the Birchfield Boiler Company shipyard in 1941 for the U.S. Coast Guard, participated in several Olympia Harbor Days tugboat races in the mid-1980s. The tender and tug was operated on the Columbia River by the U.S. Coast Guard for 35 years until decommissioned and sold as surplus to Pete Whittier in 1976. Following major restoration and refitting, the *Blueberry* was used for recreational cruising in Puget Sound and British Columbia. In the painting above by Karla Fowler from Whittier's collection, the tug is shown as she appeared during a Harbor Days race. Although the collision in the photograph below between *Blueberry* and the tug *Merilyn* at the Harbor Days race starting line looks serious, neither tug suffered any major damage. (Above, courtesy Karla Fowler; below, photograph by Mel Fredeen, courtesy Mark Freeman.)

HISTORIC TUG TWOSOME. Two restored and still-operating historic Foss tugs, the *Henrietta Foss* (left) and *Elf* (below), are important parts of Puget Sound's maritime heritage. The *Henrietta* was built at the Foss Tacoma shipyard, launched in 1931, and when sold in 1985 was the company's last active wooden tug. The painting at left by Karla Fowler of the *Henrietta* underway was purchased by Shannon Foss Bauhofer and presented to her late mother Henryetta, or "Tooty" as she was known by many. The *Elf* was built in Tacoma in 1902 and was operated as the *Foss No. 15* under Foss company ownership from 1916 to 1970. She is shown below at Olympia Harbor Days in 1988 when owned by Steve Tate. She celebrated her centennial in 2002 under owners Earl and Karen Van Diest. (Both courtesy Karla Fowler.)

Model and Miniature Tugs. The enthusiasm for tugboats throughout Puget Sound comes in many sizes. The photograph above shows three radio-controlled modelers with part of their personal tugboat fleets. From left to right are Jim Elder, who is seen with his model tug *Chris Foss*; Vic Lanza, with his tractor tug *Henry Foss;* and Jerry Julian, with his model of the *Tioga.* The popular model tugs, barges, cranes, and other equipment are demonstrated in portable ponds during various community maritime events around the Sound. A little larger but still a very small tug, the *Smitty J* is shown below being piloted by its builder, Bob Peck of Tumwater, Washington. Peck built the 10-foot-long, 13-horsepower, engine-equipped tug in his garage and exhibited and demonstrated it during Harbor Days events in the mid- and late 2000s. (Above, courtesy Chuck Fowler; below, Karla Fowler.)

RACING SMALL TUGS. Two small tugs, both under 16 feet long, square off in against each other during the 1982 Olympia Harbor Days tugboat races. The tug in the foreground is Fremont Tugboat Company's *Barf*, skippered by future tug captain Erik Freeman when he was 12 years old. The *Snapper*, owned by Bill Francis and shown with his young son Charlie at the wheel, challenged the *Barf*, but Erik won the race. (Courtesy Mark Freeman.)

TIGHTLY PACKED TUGS. At the head of Puget Sound in Olympia, this image shows vintage tugs packed tightly at Percival Landing dock during Harbor Days in the 1980s. The Percival Landing site on Labor Day weekend is a favorite end of summer gathering place for tugboat owners, captains, crews, and friends. With tugboat tours and races, shoreside arts, crafts, food vendors, and continuous entertainment, the more than three-decade-old event is popular with Olympia-area residents as well as visitors. (Courtesy Karla Fowler.)

Tug Race Tradition. Two large evenly matched vintage tugboats, the *Palomar* (above, left) and *Merilyn* (above, right), charge down the more than mile-long Harbor Days racecourse on Budd Inlet north of Olympia. Still able to top 10 knots in race competition at the ends of their careers, both tugs worked more than 50 years on Puget Sound and also participated in maritime events and tug races. A legendary T-shirt (right), produced by longtime tug engineer and former Harbor Days Harbormaster "Tiny" Freeman, not related to Mark, is being worn by former *Sand Man* owner Bob Powell during the Olympia festival. While many tug owners and captains say that winning races doesn't matter, hulls are often cleaned and painted and engines tuned in the quest for bragging rights. (Above, photograph by Scott Schoch, courtesy Mark Freeman; at right, Karla Fowler.)

TUG MEET TURNOUT. The International Retired Tugboat Association (IRTA) was formed officially in 1972. Its purpose was to allow the owners of former and some still-working tugboats and their families to gather on a regular basis to share information, swap stories, socialize, and just have fun. Membership is open to owners of tugs located primarily in Washington state and British Columbia but also to others interested in tugs beyond the region. The photograph above shows a group of six tugs rafted together in Gig Harbor in 1986 for an IRTA tug "meet." In the 1974 photograph below, families gather for a potluck supper on the aft deck of the tug *Queen* with the classic tug *Raccoon* alongside. (Both courtesy Robin Paterson.)

TUG RESTORATION BEGINS. A good example of the restoration and conversion of a retired tugboat is the major makeover of the *Joe*, the former *Joe Foss* built in 1942 in Tacoma and the Foss yard. After being sold as surplus by the Foss Maritime Company in 1972, going through two owners and a name change to *Little Toot*, the tug was purchased by Robin and Kae Paterson of Gig Harbor in 1986. Here as the first step in the tug's conversion to both a cruising and a working tug, the wheelhouse of the original trunk cabin (above) is hoisted off the deck by crane (right). This phase of the work was completed in Gig Harbor. (Both courtesy Robin Paterson.)

New Cabin Conversion. Renamed *Joe* as a link to the tug's original Foss heritage, a new trunk cabin and wheelhouse were designed by master boatbuilder Al Glaser and constructed in 1987 at his Eagle Harbor shop on Bainbridge Island. Glaser is shown above at work inside the cabin with Kae Paterson observing. As seen below, the spacious new cabin with excellent visibility was lowered onto *Joe's* deck in the same year. Glaser also designed and built the small tug *Barf* for Fremont Tugboat and his own beautifully designed 26-foot-long tug *Atka* for personal and family use. (Both courtesy Robin Paterson.)

Joe and the Patersons. Robin and Kae Paterson are shown above in 2004 aboard their restored and converted tugboat *Joe*. During the past 40 years, the Patersons have owned and restored four retired tugs: the *Bayburn; Sound*, the former *Carl Foss*; *Winamac;* and *Joe*. Robin is a U.S. Coast Guard veteran, a retired deputy sheriff, and the longtime president of the International Retired Tugboat Association. In addition to cruising, he continues to use *Joe* for towing projects throughout the Sound, and as shown below it serves as the unofficial assist tug for the historic Mosquito Fleet steamer *Virginia V*. (Above, courtesy Chuck Fowler; below, Karla Fowler.)

TUGS AND STEAMER. A traditional highlight of the annual Olympia Harbor Days festival is the participation of the steamer *Virginia V.* Built in Lisabuela on Vashon Island in 1922, she is the last of the Mosquito Fleet passenger and cargo steamboats that crisscrossed Puget Sound from the late 1800s into the 1930s. She is shown above with the tugboats *Maggie B.* from Camano Island and Dunlap Towing Company's *Cedar King*, which was built and based in Olympia. The working tugboat *Judi* M, the former *Shannon Foss* and owned by Manke Tug and Barge of Shelton, and the *Olmsted*, a retired and now live-aboard tug owned by Giles Snydor and Tracy Wang, are seen in the photograph below moored quietly at Olympia's Percival Landing following the annual Harbor Days festival. (Both courtesy Karla Fowler.)

Breaking Bow Waves. The vintage tugboats *Winamac*, built in British Columbia in 1912, and *Teal* are shown with big bow waves during an Olympia Harbor Days race in the mid-1980s. At the time, the *Winamac* was owned by Robin and Kae Paterson of Gig Harbor, and the *Teal*, built in 1949 for the Alaska Packing Company, was owned by Don Leonard of Tacoma. (Photograph by Scott Schoch, courtesy Mark Freeman.)

Historic *Arthur*. The most historic, well-known tugboat in Puget Sound is the *Arthur Foss*, shown here in late 1985. The iconic tug was built in 1889, the same year that Washington state was admitted to the Union and the year the Foss company was established. The tug was selected as one of three Washington Centennial Flagships in 1989. Retired by Foss in 1968, she has been owned and exhibited since 1970 by Northwest Seaport in Seattle as a museum vessel. (Courtesy Karla Fowler.)

BOW TO BOW. When large waves form at the stems of ships, boats, and especially blunt-bowed tugs when under full power, it is called having a "bone in her teeth" in nautical terms. This is the *Retriever*, a well-known tugboat of the Puget Sound Tug and Barge Company and part of the Cowley Maritime Corporation, as it races against the historic *Arthur Foss* during the 1981 tugboat race held in Olympia. Races are also held annually in Seattle and formerly in Tacoma. (Photograph by Scott Schoch, courtesy Mark Freeman.)

FERRY ASSIST. Two Crowley Maritime tugs, the 87-foot-long, 2,000-horsepower *Hercules* in the foreground and the *Sea Breeze* in the background, are shown in Seattle in the 1980s assisting an Issaquah-class ferryboat operated by Washington State Ferries, which is part of the Washington State Department of Transportation. Historically and currently, ship assistance is a major harbor service role for Puget Sound tugboats. (Courtesy Crowley Maritime.)

HISTORIC BATTLESHIP TOW. As shown here, the appropriately named 150-foot-long Crowley tugboat *Sea Victory* towed the historic battleship USS *Missouri* from the Puget Sound Naval Shipyard in Bremerton 2,300 miles across the Pacific Ocean to Honolulu in 1998. She was to be moored in Pearl Harbor adjacent to the USS *Arizona* Memorial to honor the thousands of sailors and soldiers who were killed as a result of the enemy attack in 1941, which brought the United States into World War II. At the war's end, the surrender papers were signed by the Japanese aboard the *Missouri*. Except for periods when recalled to active duty during the Korean and Persian Gulf wars, she was part of the inactive ship fleet at Bremerton and on public exhibit for more than 50 years. (Courtesy Crowley Maritime.)

Seattle Tugboat Races. The first official tugboat race in Puget Sound was staged in Tacoma in conjunction with the premiere of the 1933 movie *Tugboat Annie*. Seattle periodically presented workboat races, including tugs beginning in the late 1930s through the mid-1950s and then in 1979. Resurrected in 1985, the Seattle races promoted in the 2008 poster above are part of the annual Maritime Week event and have become the largest in Puget Sound and the world. (Courtesy Hamilton/Saunderson.)

Tug Enthusiasts Tour. Members of the Tugboat Enthusiasts of the Americas are shown here in 1997 touring the Crowley Maritime tug *Hunter* on the Seattle waterfront. The group held its annual meeting in the Pacific Northwest and toured and rode on tugs in Seattle, Tacoma, Olympia, and Portland. The Olympia visit included rides during the Harbor Days tug races. (Courtesy Crowley Maritime.)

Raging Tug Race. With the Seattle skyline in the background, the Crowley tugboat *Hunter* leads other unlimited-class tugs competing in the 1999 Maritime Week races. The 136-foot-long *Hunter*, powered by 7,200-total-horsepower diesel engines, has been a perennial tug race winner on Elliott Bay for many years. Tugs from companies large and small, educational institutions such as the Seattle Maritime Academy, nonprofit groups such as Northwest Seaport, and the Steamer *Virginia V* Foundation participate in the popular annual event. In the beginning, three tugboats participated in the second Seattle workboat race held in 1939, but racing was suspended through the World War II years in the early 1940s. Races were run from 1949 to 1955 and in 1979; they were reinstated permanently in 1985 as a highlight of Maritime Week. The annual event is sponsored by the Port of Seattle, the Seattle Propeller Club, and many other maritime industry and waterfront organizations. (Courtesy Crowley Maritime.)

PROTECTOR TUGBOAT. The Crowley Maritime tugboat *Protector*, shown above and below operating on Seattle's Elliott Bay, was one of two new 120-foot-long, 5,500-total-horsepower tractor tugs introduced in 1996 and designed specifically for large ship escort and docking work. As part of its escort and protection role, the photograph above shows the tug's firefighting capability as both fire monitor nozzles are demonstrated. The pump for each monitor is capable of pumping 6,600 gallons of water per minute for fire emergencies. In the photograph below, the *Protector's* rounded hull design coupled with its Voith-Schneider cycloidal propulsion system allows flexible ship-assist maneuvers, and the high wheelhouse provides maximum master-operator visibility. (Courtesy Crowley Maritime.)

New Design Tugs. The 1980s and 1990s saw new design innovations and changes in the Pacific Coast tugboat industry, including Puget Sound. Crowley Maritime introduced the Harbor Series of 105-foot-long tractor tugs with the launching of the *Master* in 1998. Constructed by Nichols Brothers Boat Builders of Freeland, Washington, on Whidbey Island, a total of six of the class, including the *Leader* (above), were built during 1998 and 1999. Each tug is powered by twin Caterpillar diesels producing a total of 4,800 horsepower. Another new design tug, the *Tioga* (below), was acquired from the Coos Bay Tugboat Company in 1998. After several assignments in Los Angeles, Long Beach, and San Francisco, the tug was reassigned in 2007 to Puget Sound for ship assist work in Seattle and Tacoma. (Courtesy Crowley Maritime.)

WATERFRONT WORKBOATS. One of the Manson Construction Company's early tugboats was the 38-foot-long converted former government freight boat *Myrtle May*, shown above, which was purchased in 1928. The Manson tugboat fleet grew with the company and more than 20 tugs have supported marine construction projects during more than a century of operation. The 60-foot-long *Wollochet*, shown below on the Seattle waterfront in 1997, is a triple-screw or propeller tug powered by three diesel engines totaling 1,450 horsepower. Very maneuverable, the tugboat was purchased in 1995 and is used to tow and shift pile drivers, barges, and other construction support equipment for various projects. (Courtesy Manson Construction.)

MUSCLE TOWBOATS. A former U.S. Navy freight vessel was purchased by Manson and was converted in 1975 to the multi-deck *Harry M*, the company's largest ocean-going towboat. The 98-foot-long muscle towboat, shown at right moving a pile-driver crane barge, is powered by twin 1,500-horsepower General Motors diesel engines. The difference between a towboat and a tugboat is that towboats primarily push barges and other floating equipment and tugboats tow from a bitt or tow winch located at the stern. The heavily built 90-foot-long *Peter M*, the third workboat to bear the company founder's name, was launched in 1998 and has 4,000-horsepower and a Z-drive Kort nozzle propeller propulsion system. She was designed by naval architect Bob Long and built at Fisherman's Boat Shop in Seattle. (Both courtesy Manson Construction.)

MILITARY VETERANS. Many former military tugboats, both large and small, have been converted to successful working commercial tugboats. Shown above is *Spike* with a "bone in her teeth" bow wave during a tugboat race. She was owned during the 1980s by Global Diving and Salvage Company of Seattle. The 65-foot-long tug was built for U.S. Navy marine support service as a YTL or small harbor tug and was used by Global Diving and Salvage Company to move diving barges, oil spill containment containers, and other equipment throughout Puget Sound. The 45-foot-long tugboat *Reliable*, shown below, is a surplus U.S. Army ST (Small Tug) and was owned and operated by Phil Shiveley of Shiveley Towing Company in the 1980s and early 1990s. The 165-horsepower tug won several Olympia Harbor Days tug races. (Both courtesy Mark Freeman.)

COMPANY TUGS. Many independent companies operate tugboats throughout Puget Sound—both from Seattle and other homeports. Above is the former U.S. Navy tug *Patricia S.* in the foreground overtaking the *Helen S.* that is towing a barge on the Duwamish River in Seattle in the 1980s. Both were owned by Island Tug and Barge Company, which was established in 1979 with towing operations in Puget Sound, Alaska, the Pacific Coast, and the Western Hemisphere. Another independent, family-owned tug company, with headquarters in La Conner in north Puget Sound, is Dunlap Towing. It was established in 1926. The company owns a fleet of tugs that range from 36 to 110 feet long and operated the now retired 100-foot-long *Skagit Chief*, shown below. (Both courtesy Mark Freeman.)

Big Barge; Small Tugs. In this 1989 photograph, the Dunlap Towing Company harbor tug *Camano* is towing a large barge with two small tugs aboard. The barge was used for assignments in Alaska and here it is on its way into the Hiram Chittenden Locks in Seattle's Ballard district to be loaded at the Northland Services terminal. (Courtesy Mark Freeman.)

Tug in Art. The former Manke Tug and Barge Company tugboat *Sigrid H.* is depicted with a taut tow line in this striking painting by Pacific Northwest marine artist Marshall Johnson. Formerly the U.S. Army *ST-2198*, built in 1955, the 65-foot-long tug towed logs and barges in Alaska and on the Sound for Boyer Towing and then Manke from 1987 to 2006. (Courtesy Marshall Johnson.)

BRIDGE TOW. As part of the construction of the new $849-million Tacoma Narrows Bridge, the 590-foot-long heavy-lift ship *Swan* brought the bridge's deck sections from Seoul, South Korea, to Puget Sound beginning in 2006. Here the 5,750-horsepower Crowley Maritime Sea Swift–class tug *Mars* tows the *Swan* under the bridge so the individual sections, which are 120 feet long, 78 feet wide, and 30 feet high, can be hoisted to the bridge roadway level above. (Photograph by Mike Stork, courtesy Kathie Stork.)

TITAN TUGBOAT. This is the Western Towboat Company's tractor tug *Alaska Titan* in a floating dry dock as she was towed by the tug *Wasp* into Lake Union for launching in 2008. The 120-foot-long, 5,000-horsepower tug was the fifth in a series of new ocean-going tugboats built by Western for their Seattle-to-Alaska towing service. A family-owned business since 1948, Western provides tug and barge towing services from Puget Sound to Alaska and the North Pacific, Hawaiian Islands, and the Gulf of Mexico. The massive tandem propellers in Kort nozzles on the *Alaska Titan* can rotate 360 degrees to provide outstanding maneuverability. Z-drive propulsion units transfer power from the twin diesel engines to the propellers. (Both courtesy Mark Freeman.)

High-Tech Tractor Tugs. The *Pacific Star*, shown above passing under the Aurora or George Washington Memorial Bridge in Seattle, and the *America*, seen below on sea trials on Commencement Bay in Tacoma, became the newest tractor tugs in the Foss Maritime fleet in 2008. Leased from Signet Maritime, both are 98 feet long, powered by twin 3,300-horsepower diesel engines, feature Z-drive and Kort nozzle propulsion units, and are highly maneuverable. The high-tech tugs were constructed by J. M. Martinac Shipbuilding of Tacoma, which has been building commercial fish boats, military craft, tugboats, and other vessels in Puget Sound since 1924. (Above, courtesy Mark Freeman; below, photograph by Mike Stork, courtesy Kathie Stork.)

Cruise Port Tug Racing. Puget Sound's 75-year tradition of tugboat racing and festivals allow the public to see tugboats in action and provides a window on the towing industry and its many important aspects. The 2007 Seattle tugboat races provided one of these windows when the Crowley Maritime tugboat *Gladiator* (right foreground) and the Foss Maritime tug *Craig Foss* (left foreground) power past the Norwegian Cruise Line ship *Norwegian Star* along the downtown waterfront on Elliott Bay. These events in Seattle, Olympia, and Tacoma (in

the past) allow the public to tour tugs, talk to captains and crew members, and learn more about the important role of tugboats, barges, and other related equipment in the marine-related economy of Pacific Northwest. And they help generate lasting legacy interest in this colorful, cooperative—but also very competitive—aspect of Puget Sound maritime history. (Photograph by Don Wilson, courtesy Port of Seattle.)